ANTIC

The MIT Press Essential Knowledge Series

A complete list of the titles in this series appears at the back of this book.

ANTICORRUPTION

ROBERT I. ROTBERG

The MIT Press | Cambridge, Massachusetts | London, England

This book was set in Chaparral Pro by Toppan Best-set Premedia Limited. Printed and bound in the United States of America.

Library of Congress Cataloging-in-Publication Data

Names: Rotberg, Robert I., author.
Title: Anticorruption / Robert I. Rotberg.
Description: Cambridge, Massachusetts : The MIT Press, [2020] | Series: The MIT Press essential knowledge series | Includes bibliographical references and index.
Identifiers: LCCN 2019032467 | ISBN 9780262538831 (paperback)
Subjects: LCSH: Political corruption—ase studies. | Political corruption—Prevention—Case studies.
Classification: LCC JF1081 .R6827 2020 | DDC 364.1/323—dc23
LC record available at https://lccn.loc.gov/2019032467

10   9   8   7   6   5   4   3   2   1

CONTENTS

SERIES FOREWORD

The MIT Press Essential Knowledge series offers accessible, concise, beautifully produced pocket-size books on topics of current interest. Written by leading thinkers, the books in this series deliver expert overviews of subjects that range from the cultural and the historical to the scientific and the technical.

In today's era of instant information gratification, we have ready access to opinions, rationalizations, and superficial descriptions. Much harder to come by is the foundational knowledge that informs a principled understanding of the world. Essential Knowledge books fill that need. Synthesizing specialized subject matter for nonspecialists and engaging critical topics through fundamentals, each of these compact volumes offers readers a point of access to complex ideas.

Corruption is an insidious cancer of nearly all bodies politic. Corrupt practices harshly cut across classes and castes, disturb institutions, destroy communities, and infect the very structure of people's lives. Corruption corrodes nations, even the most advanced, and saps their moral fiber. Moreover, corruption is invasive and unforgiving. It degrades governance, distorts and criminalizes national priorities, and privileges skimming natural resource wealth, patrimonial theft, and personal and family gains over concern for the commonweal.

Much of the globe is infected with corruption, sapping as much as 3 percent of annual per capita GDP in large swathes of Africa, Asia, and Latin America. Even North America is hardly immune. The World Bank says that $1 trillion or more is lost each year to corruption, globally.[1]

The corruption complaint has become central to citizens' concerns almost everywhere in the world. Charges and countercharges surge across social media; politicians accuse their competitors of corrupt behavior. Elections are regularly contested with corruption as a fundamental theme, as we have seen recently in such diverse nations as Argentina, Brazil, Canada, El Salvador, Hungary, India, Israel, Italy, Kenya, Malawi, Mexico, Nigeria, Pakistan,

South Africa, Thailand, Zambia, and Zimbabwe. Cries against corruption in national political life are also heard in China and the United States. Corruption, in sum, is among the key overriding issues of our age.

Conquering corruption, or at least moderating political or corporate corrupt behavior, helps underprivileged peoples to prosper and to begin to experience substantially better human outcomes. Combating corruption is among the important initiatives that materially strengthens overall human outcomes.

Fortunately, we now know how best to battle against corruption, and what measures work and what ones do not. We know that altering collective behavior provides lasting answers to the corrupt imperative. We also know now that committed leadership is critical to drives against corruption. Strengthened institutions come after national leaders have enunciated and presided over an emerging political culture antithetical to continued corruption. That is, institutions alone cannot counter corrupt practices unless leaders exercising political will have socialized their citizens to accept a political culture of probity. This book sets out these propositions at length, and argues against older theories of how and why corruption exists, the primacy of institutions, and how corruption can best be diminished in public and corporate life.

This addition to the Essential Knowledge book series characterizes the various destructive practices of corruption worldwide, and epitomizes how corrupt practices have been and can be reduced. Ideally, this book will serve as a Baedeker for reformers as well as opinion shapers and opinion makers. It is written for the informed general reader, but also for scholars and researchers, and for students who want to understand the dangerous ills of our modern society and how best to remedy them.

This book's first chapter explains what corruption is, in theory and practice, and how scholars and practitioners have described the affliction and its baleful consequences. The second chapter discusses how we measure corruption, and thus how we compare countries against each other in terms of their respective amounts of corruption. The third chapter explains how the Nordic nations, New Zealand, and Canada, now all rated among the least corrupt in the world, were once overflowing with corrupt practices, and how those were moderated and then largely extinguished. Chapter 4 extends the examination of how nations shifted from the corrupt to the noncorrupt sides of the ledger in South America and Central America, and particularly to the modern cases of Uruguay, Chile, and Costa Rica, the least corrupt governments in Latin America.

Chapter 5 begins a detailed series of analyses about the role of various kinds of legal and judicial systems in curtailing corruption. Chapter 6 looks at the role of auditors, ombudspersons, investigative free media, and other exemplifications of transparency and accountability. It also discusses the difference between public and private corruption, and how multinational corporations can become effective antagonists of corrupt behavior. Chapter 7 shows how accountability can be enhanced through the use of technological advances, such as cell phones, webcams, blockchains, biometrics, opinion polling, and the like.

The eighth chapter of the book details a strong case that responsible political leadership is essential to combat corruption successfully. Without sufficient political will—a hitherto-understudied component—and wise disruptions of existing societal patterns, corruption simply continues. Since corruption starts from the top, good political leadership matters, especially in the United States, which is discussed. The final chapter of the book draws from the eighth and earlier chapters to provide a bold thirteen-step recipe for anticorruption success.

This book builds constructively on my *The Corruption Cure* (2017) and my edited "Anticorruption: How to Beat Back Political and Corporate Corruption," which was a special issue of *Daedalus* (2018). Both volumes advance detailed arguments about how to struggle against the abiding curse of corruption and to reduce its toll on the globe's peoples. This book—and those earlier efforts—examines what has worked against the corrupt disorder in the past (even in nineteenth-century Scandinavia and the antipodes) and the varied policies that are succeeding now in a few exemplary modern countries. It discusses the central roles in anticorruption endeavors of governance and leadership, investigative commissions and free media, judicial independence and strong rules of law, corporate integrity, international institutions and legal arrangements, and innovative technological solutions.

R. I. R.
January 10, 2020

ACKNOWLEDGMENTS

The MIT Press, with which I have been associated for a half century as a journal editor and critic, smartly created its Essential Knowledge book series. I am honored to have been asked to include this extended treatment of one of the key economic, social, and political complexities of our era in such an esteemed addition to readership and learning. I thank Emily Taber, particularly, for her exacting editorial oversight of this book. Three anonymous reviewers provided insightful readings and critiques that greatly improved the book and its overall argument.

Peter Eigen, founder of Transparency International and several innovative anticorruption organizations such as the Extractive Industries Transparency Initiative (EITI), years ago helped significantly to shine incandescent light on the corrosive qualities of corruption globally, and to lay critical foundations for this and many other anticorruption endeavors. This book salutes his persistent and formative influence on those of us who try to follow in his big footsteps.

Although they have had no direct connection with the composition of this book, I acknowledge with great pleasure the profound scholarship and pathbreaking ideas of my learned colleagues Alina Mungiu-Pippidi and

Bo Rothstein, and the exceptional pioneering research of Susan Rose-Ackerman. Their dedicated attempts to advance the study of corruption in all of its complexity are among the most important of the many intellectual foundations on which this book and the *Daedalus* volume rest. Each contributed significant essays to that special issue, as did Matthew Taylor, who has instructed me helpfully and well about South American corruption. The writings of all three (and others) are noted in the "Further Reading" section of this book.

I have learned much from these and many other scholars as well as from a host of other writers and practitioners, especially from such frontline stalwarts as Justice Richard Goldstone of South Africa and Judge Mark L. Wolf of the United States. We should all be indebted, as I am, to those who continue to fight against fraud, graft, money laundering, and extortion in public and private life. As President Theodore Roosevelt thundered, "No man who is corrupt, no man who condones corruption in others, can possibly do his duty by the community."[1]

CORRUPTION: ITS ESSENCE

Corruption is contorted, obscured, and often devious, but its underlying origins are rarely hard to understand. Corruption is the conversion of a societal good—a communal good—into personal gain. As India officially legislated in 2018, it is the gaining of "advantage" illicitly. It is the obtaining of "influence" through underhand payments or promises of reciprocal rewards. Usually, corruption is denominated monetarily: How much has a corrupt politician or official stolen from the people? In many countries, cash-filled brown envelopes still change hands. Overinvoicing, construction projects that are paid for yet never completed, and the hiring of nonexistent employees are but a few of the ways that such outright theft is managed. Persons of power can also corruptly favor syndicates or corporations—or even foreign political entities—by proffering them influence and special access that is against the public interest, and without explicit transfers of cash. Corruption bends policies meant to be for all to benefit the few.

"Getting things done" is a frequent rationalization of corruption. But underlying corrupt attempts to gain advantage over others or gain preferment of some kind is something basic to the human species, or even all primates: greed. Another motive is "getting what others get" or not losing advantage to others. No one likes to be disadvantaged or to be thought of "as a fool" for not benefiting from easily available perquisites, or at least the favors that similarly placed persons are gaining licitly or illicitly. A police person on the beat looks to see what his or her colleagues are doing. If others are "getting away" with sleaze, he or she usually want to do the same. If one state trooper figures out a way to take advantage of his/ her position by overbilling for hours or taking payoffs from vendors, others will want to emulate such a "clever" entrepreneur.

Greed, in other words, is hardwired into the human condition. Corrupt acts therefore flow from a natural, even rational urge to improve one's status and earnings. Both the giver and taker of exchanges that are fundamentally corrupt seek to improve their places in the universe, their rents and wages, their places in the queue of rewards, and even their introductions to positions and persons of power.

Corruption is deeply based on reciprocity, the cultivation of mutual favors, gift giving and taking, and something more tangible than a mere handshake or verbal promise. Corruption contains acknowledgments of power, primacy, and what well-placed individuals can do, and how they can assist less fortunate or less well-placed individuals. Or sometimes it demonstrates the crude conceits of dominance, control, and rewards.

The processes of corruption oil whatever wheels permit the vehicles of life and the governmental-citizen engine to roll faster, to roll in a preferred direction, to roll more surely, and to roll at all. In these last senses, corruption is a method of allocating scarce or purposely scarce resources to the highest bidders (not the most deserving). Corruption can minimize disadvantages based on status, class, color, or religion, and partially overcome discriminatory behavior visited on, say, a minority or an ethnicity. An ethnic Chinese Malaysian or a mixed-heritage Thai businessperson can remedy any impediments to corporate success by paying substantially for permits or licenses otherwise only available to indigenous persons, but the unequal system still remains in place. That is what has long occurred in Southeast Asia, where majority populations have denied equal opportunities to minorities of other ethnic backgrounds. The latter traditionally have regained lost privileges and chances to prosper by quietly rewarding those in power.[1]

Definitions

The standard definition of corruption is "the abuse of public office for private gain." Transparency International and others expand that all-purpose definition by explaining that abuses of "the public trust," not just abuses of public office, are corrupt. Thus, when FIFA officials undermined the level fields of bidding for the World Cup and other regional contests, these were abuses of the public trust even though no FIFA board member or official had been elected to "public" office.

These definitions are widely accepted by scholars, practitioners, and government officials. None is contested. Nor nowadays do commentators argue against the universality of these definitions. Every country has laws that outlaw corruption, as defined here. No jurisdiction condones corrupt acts.

Given abuses of either public office (narrowly or broadly construed) or the public trust, it is obvious that corrupt acts include asking for or receiving bribes (whether those that are employed to gain a good or service, intended to accelerate service delivery, or arranged to deprive others of benefits or property), extortion (coerced bribes or payments in kind), kickbacks (a form of extortion in which contracts are overinvoiced so that there is room for contractual profits and payments to those who decide who wins the fake bids), embezzlement (blatant theft from the public purse), nepotism (giving a rewarding position or contract to a relative rather than allowing a meritorious or competitive exercise to take place), padding salary rolls with "ghost" workers, graft (awarding public contracts without honest competition), paying hush money or blackmail, and arbitrarily appropriating public resources for private use. Each of these and many other corrupt acts involve deceit. Each evades accountability and transparency.

In classical as well as modern times, a bribe was and is universally shameful, never acknowledged publicly, and illegal in every jurisdiction.[2] Governmental decisions have always represented something valuable to some or several citizens. Without that value there would be little corruption.[3] Whenever a public official deviates from an accepted norm and serves herself, that is blatant and obvious corrupt dealing, even or particularly when it is common and customary.

Corruption indicates that a state, public body, or corporation is not functioning as fully as it was intended to function. Instead of delivering appropriate levels of service, called "good governance," if the jurisdiction is governmental, these corrupt bodies are focusing on supplying rents or emoluments to persons in charge. (Rents are any payment to an owner in excess of the costs needed to produce a certain item. Emoluments are illicit profits or fees from an office, employment, or sale.) A corrupted

In classical as well as modern times, a bribe was and is universally shameful, never acknowledged publicly, and illegal in every jurisdiction.

governmental apparatus at any level consequently thus forfeits its legitimacy as a neutral, all-encompassing, and beneficial provider of services to its citizens and taxpayers, or its shareholders and consumers, and becomes a vehicle for illicit personal enrichment.

Corruption occurs when public servants or corporate leaders disregard their obligations to operate for the commonweal, and make special arrangements for private profiteering. As Cicero long ago suggested, corruption is a betrayal of fidelity to the public interest. Or it is a "subversion" of the public interest. Biographer James Bosworth's Samuel Johnson called corruption "wickedness; perversion of principles." "Mankind," opined Johnson, "are universally corrupt." More recent commentators call corruption "a moral evil"—a breach of duty.[4]

Public officials of all kinds, even those who run such organizations as the International Olympic Committee, have an obligation to be impartial. At least that is the common expectation. When they do not—when they behave with partiality by discriminating in favor of one person or group against others, and by gaining personal rewards or misbehaving in that manner—those officials are corrupt and corrupted. They are not observing distributional justice. As the late Singaporean prime minister and nation builder Lee Kuan Yew said, "There must be a level playing field for all."[5] That is what citizens regard as "fair."

As Cicero long ago suggested, corruption is a betrayal of fidelity to the public interest.

When public and private officials put their own undue personal interests ahead of the stated public interest, those norm deviations are corrupt. Doing so cheats the public, erodes the legitimacy of the polity involved, coarsens discourse between the state (or municipality or corporation) and the citizen or consumer, invites cynicism, and distorts priorities. No political jurisdiction can function on behalf of its citizens and stakeholders if its leaders and middle managers are focused on private gain rather than public enrichment. Instead, bridges collapse, roads crumble, food is tainted, organs are peddled for profit, police self-enrich at roadblocks, marriage and birth certificates become costly, and the very fundamentals of a safe and secure life are compromised.

The Criminal State

In many parts of the world, criminal elements merge with the executive leadership. That is, the state (or a province) is captured by persons or syndicates who use corrupt officials and politicians as well as the corrupted state to enrich enterprises established to loot for profit. Russia and several of the former Soviet states in central Asia are regimes that are at least criminalized, if not criminal. Governments of Afghanistan have depended on a steady flow of corrupt earnings. "Every government position is bought; even promotions in the army and police depend on patronage and purchase."[6] Money flows illicitly from US security forces and contractors, foreign assistance, and foreign militaries, via Afghan officials and corrupt Afghan intermediaries, straight to the Taliban. Otherwise, ordinary logistics would be disrupted, transport curtailed, and many reciprocal indigenous relations of long standing imperiled. "We [the US] just poured so much money into [Afghanistan] we contributed to the corruption problem, we were like throwing fuel on the fire," concluded John F. Sopko, the US special inspector general for Afghanistan reconstruction.[7]

The situation is much the same in Mexico, where narcotics trafficking syndicates have long been intertwined with national and state political parties and governments. South Africa was "captured" by an Indian-originated troika of thieves from one family in cahoots with the national president and his family and cronies. Criminal entrepreneurs and politicians worked together for mutual enrichment in Honduras and Guatemala. Former UN ambassador Nikki Haley explained that corruption wasn't just part of the system of dysfunction in many of the countries on the Security Council's watch list; it *was* "the system." In places like Venezuela, she declared, governments do not exist to serve their people; they exist to serve themselves and their leaders, "and corruption is the means by which they do so."[8] Even in Canada, otherwise regarded as little corrupt, biddings for municipal and provincial contracts have been rigged in criminal ways, according to the findings of the authoritative Charbonneau Commission.

Universal Condemnation

Elected and unelected officials, and even heads of private and public corporations, know better. In no international jurisdiction is corruption legal. Indeed, the United Nations, the Organization for Economic Cooperation and Development, the African Union, the European Union, the Organization of American States, the Association of Southeast Asian Nations, and many other international and all national bodies explicitly condemn corruption. Many wide-ranging academic investigations have confirmed that there are no societies that approve corruption; those traditional cultures that accept gift exchanges still expect them to be transparent.

Because of an underlying propensity to be greedy, and because the human condition seeks advantage, there is no shortage of corruption in the contemporary universe. Moreover, corruption is an ancient phenomenon, experienced by Mesopotamians and everyone since. Well-born and common citizens have always sought preferment. Powerful individuals in early eras recognized that being a gatekeeper conferred advantages that could be transformed into substantial private wealth. Gatekeepers then and now could be "persuaded" to give advantage for "a consideration." Ancient Indian epics speak explicitly of bribery to keep the devil at bay. Dutch high officeholders in the eighteenth century sold rewarding public positions and pocketed the proceeds while the buyers (and new officeholders) fleeced the public. So did eighteenth-century Danes and nineteenth-century Americans, Britons, and Canadians. A nineteenth-century Canadian prime minister sold permits for railway construction regularly and kept the extra returns for himself alone. A twenty-first-century president of Guatemala took Chinese money to divest his country of ties to Taiwan and ran off with the result. A court in the same nation sentenced its former vice president to fifteen years in prison for defrauding the state on behalf of a foreign chemical concern. Countries and contractors have always been willing to pay for results, no matter how questionably obtained.

Plato, Aristotle, Ibn Khaldun, Thomas Hobbes, George Eliot, and a plethora of commentators in all times and periods have recognized that corruption is odious as well as disruptive. President Theodore Roosevelt, the first US high office holder to campaign against corruption early in the twentieth century, declared that the practice of corruption obliterated the people's government. "If we put corrupt men in public office," he thundered, and "sneeringly acquiesce in their corruptions, then we are wrong ourselves."[9]

Baleful Consequences

Corruption inhibits improved health outcomes and educational opportunities almost everywhere. In Malawi, a minister of education purchased millions of expensive textbooks unsuitable for classroom use. He pocketed the kickbacks, and students lost the chance to learn. A more recent case of outrageous kickbacks occurred in Nigeria, where two British-based oil exploration entrepreneurs connived with local partners to receive 15 percent of a $300 million deal, defrauding their own shareholders and the Nigerian government for private benefit (the purchase of luxurious homes on Caribbean islands).

Corruption's persistence in public and private life even leads to losses of life; deaths from natural disasters could have been avoided if national rules and regulations had not been breached for private gain, as in civil conflicts in Africa and Asia that arise because of regime-inflicted avarice or scrambles for illicit resources. The massive destruction caused in Kathmandu, for example, after the 2016 earthquake that destroyed large parts of the Nepali capital, depended on corruptly acquired permits to evade building regulations. The chemical explosion that maimed thousands in Tianjin, China, resulted from bribes to elude strict rules. Corrupt interference with the supply of antiretroviral medicines doomed Ukrainian HIV/AIDS patients to perish. Measles and infantile paralysis vaccination campaigns in Asia and Africa are interrupted for corrupt gains. The civil wars in the Central African Republic, the Democratic Republic of Congo, and Mali all stem in part from (excessive) corrupt dealings by successive regimes.

Corruption is intimately linked to the smuggling of narcotics, arms, migrants, and people otherwise enslaved. It facilitates the clandestine movement of nuclear materials and assists in the proliferation of nuclear weapons. It depends on and propels money laundering. The growth of transnational criminality and the rise of criminal gangs would be impossible without corruption—without surreptitious payments to government officials, military leaders, police coconspirators and informants, and more. "How can you solve the problem of violence and organized crime," a leading Mexican campaigner for better business conditions asked, "if you don't solve the problem of corruption?"[10]

Corruption has generated many of the globe's current dire security crises. Many terroristic enterprises are financed almost fully by corrupt enterprises, often connected to narcotics and other forms of smuggling. The terror wars of the African Sahel and the southern reaches of the Sahara Desert depend on corrupt proceedings in Algeria, Burkina Faso, Mali, Mauritania, and Niger. The depredations of the Somali al-Shabaab are financed by the secretive movements of drugs and charcoal, both facilitated by corruption. Boko Haram in Nigeria could not exist without corrupt gains, many from drug shipments. In Myanmar, a wide web of corruption has for years enabled the passage of opium and illicitly plundered jade to China. The wars and armies that plague that country and its Kachin, Shan, and Wa states are all dependent on a climate of corruption that for decades has enriched the national army—the Tatmadaw—and its leaders.

As mentioned earlier, the World Bank reports that $1 trillion is paid annually in bribes. Dividing this number by the planet's total population could mean that 1.6 billion persons annually give or are forced to give bribes. The World Economic Forum estimates that the annual global cost of corruption is about 5 percent of the total planetary GDP, possibly $2.6 trillion. It also says that corruption increases the cost of doing business by 10 percent, on average. Global Financial Integrity believes that $7.8 trillion was diverted illegally from the wealth of emerging economies between 2004 and 2013 through such artifices as tax evasion, embezzlement, other corrupt acts, and criminal activity.[11]

A recent study of Nigeria says that it loses 8 percent a year to corruption. Bulgaria's Center for the Study of

The World Economic Forum estimates that the annual global cost of corruption is about 5 percent of the total planetary GDP, possibly $2.6 trillion.

Democracy claims that 20 percent of that country's citizens have paid or received a bribe. RAND Europe, a think tank, reports that Bulgaria annually loses 20 percent of its total GDP to corruption. Most careful examinations of the results of corruption by economists suggest that developing nations forgo, on average, 2 percent of GDP yearly. Whatever the real figures may be, the number of persons impacted directly by corruption is enormous and the direct wages of cancerous corruption are substantial. The resulting damage to fragile economies and peoples is vast and debilitating.[12]

The indirect costs of corruption are equally debilitating and harmful. Corruption leads to low economic growth rates and rising income inequalities. National financial stability is reduced because of corruption. Debt crises are often induced and then enhanced by corruption, as in Zimbabwe during the first nineteen years of this century, Turkey in 2019, Argentina earlier in this century, and many other countries where corruption is rampant. Moreover, corruption (and weak rules of law) reduces the inflows of critically required foreign investment.

A former president of the World Bank termed corruption "the largest single inhibitor of equitable economic development." A successor as president calls corruption "Public Enemy Number One." A US secretary of state blamed corruption for foreign extremism and domestic dissent across the globe.[13]

The bottom line reached by these conscientious research findings and highly placed declarations is that corrupt acts, and a pervasive climate of corruption, costs the least well-endowed countries more than they receive, on average, from foreign aid. So corruption deepens the low-level poverty trap that already ensnares most of the world's impoverished citizens. If we could reduce what amounts to the theft of public resources by elected or self-appointed politicians, large numbers of people (in developed as well as developing countries) would benefit directly from better schooling opportunities, better health outcomes, fewer roads with potholes, less terror, fewer wars, and enhanced chances to prosper. Reduced corruption could also lead to more jobs in nations where unofficial unemployment rates range from 30 percent upward to Zimbabwe's 90 percent.

Those are among the larger impacts of corruption on whole populations around the world. At the individual level, however, most inhabitants of poor or near-poor developing countries are afflicted by interactions with some form of authority that is intrinsically corrupt, and offensive to individuals daily. Those interactions exemplify the differences between grand or venal corruption—big-time rip-offs, contractual fraud, sell outs to foreign powers, illicit concessions to natural resource–stripping corporations, and the like—and the so-called petty corruption that penalizes the less powerful and the powerless in so many of the world's smaller and most endangered political spaces.

Petty Corruption

Petty corruption is the handing over of relatively small sums (as much as fifteen dollars every day for Kenyans) for governmental acts that should by right be available freely to all citizens. It is often a form of extortion. The official behind the grille never refuses to provide a birth certificate, marriage license, or driving permit. She simply makes it clear in perfect bureaucratese that she is much too busy to search for or stamp any documents until she is appropriately induced (rewarded). Sometimes hapless citizens are asked for "tea money." Queues are interminable; if the petitioner wants to jump the line or receive timely attention to his registration or other necessity, a "gift" to the official behind the grille becomes appropriate. Facilitation payments are the norm almost anywhere in the developing world that there are still regulations that can be interpreted by an official, or where the delivery of a service—no matter how routine—can be exploited for personal gain. That is why petty corruption is frequently labeled "lubricating" or "speedy" corruption.

Physicians or nurses in hospitals throughout much of Africa and Asia are accustomed to receiving envelopes stuffed with cash. Otherwise, attention in government and even private hospitals may be delayed or diverted. Teachers in many nations anticipate receiving gifts of cash at the beginning and end of terms as well as before holidays. Parents would not want their children to be neglected. South Korea recently barred the practice, and Georgia, when it was reforming earlier in this century, introduced procedures to make examinations more honest, forbidding cash transfers.

Roadblocks, set up by traffic police or vigilantes, are an expedient method of extorting payments from motorists attempting to proceed normally down highways or busy city streets in many African and Asian countries. At a roadblock, drivers are falsely accused of having a broken headlight, a cracked mirror, or otherwise breaching rules. A small payment, especially if it is dark out, and the police or pseudopolice are menacing, allows an automobile or a passenger bus to proceed. I had my own experience with a Constable Moyo in Zimbabwe that was contrived, petty, annoying, and costly (twenty dollars, or the equivalent to a week's pay for a laboring Zimbabwean).

In Kinshasa, the capital of the Democratic Republic of Congo, traffic cops receive 80 percent of their income from what are euphemistically called "informal tolls." Every driver must pay a protection fee to the cops. "This is done by sticking a fist out of the [car] window at certain junctions ... and dropping a note worth [thirty US cents] into a waiting policeman's hand."[14] Drivers who try to avoid this particular "squeeze" find themselves subject to large fines for (imaginary) offenses, which the police invent at will. Part of the cop's take goes to his superiors. There are daily quotas.

In Sierra Leone, offenders on trial routinely negotiate lighter sentences by paying fees to clerks and magistrates. In Sierra Leone's hospitals, even during the Ebola epidemic, nurses' handbags became illicit pharmacies from which drugs were sold to patients. No cash, no medicine.

At Nigeria's international airport, hustlers working in cahoots with security personnel slow down queues so that they can sell access to the fast-track lanes for ten dollars. Since Nigeria is a large country where its two hundred million citizens are accustomed to escalating levels of petty corruption, nearly everyone is compelled daily to endure the system or to use it for her or his own gain.

In Cambodia, it is a common sight to see truck drivers, when crossing a main bridge in the capital, throwing the equivalent of a dollar or two out of their windows so they won't have to haggle over larger bribes. In Phnom Penh, the capital, parents give sums to their children to bribe teachers to let them into class.

In Bangladesh, 71 percent of households surveyed reported that they paid bribes to obtain services of many kinds. A further 27 percent bribed officials routinely to avoid harassment and "complications." Nearly 77 percent of Bangladeshis paid to obtain a passport, 75 percent to placate the police, 61 percent to obtain a place in a school, 48 percent to influence judges, and 32 percent to get electric power installed.

This is the ordeal experienced daily across much of the world. Small sums are exchanged to avoid being hassled, to get to work on time, to complete an errand, to obtain that vital permit, or to gain a necessarily slight advantage over someone also waiting interminably in a queue or seeking attention in a hospital. Although less developmentally destructive and somewhat less wasteful in aggregate terms than the effects of grand corruption, petty corruption is still a massive waste of time and cash as well as damaging economically wherever it is common. Petty corruption also eats away at the social structure of nations, and undermines trust and governance. Routinized petty corruption is pernicious, unrelenting, and enervating.

Grand Corruption

Grand corruption hardly interferes with or impinges on the day-to-day routine activities of citizens. People go about their business, lubricating and providing speed payments whenever necessary, but without necessarily being aware of how their political or other officials are enriching themselves at their expense. Grand corruption is the large-scale theft of state privileges and opportunities for private gain. The UN Office on Drugs and Crime calls grand corruption the kind that "pervades the highest level of national government, leading to a broad erosion of confidence in good governance, the rule of law, and economic stability."[15] Grand corrupters are often called kleptocrats since kleptocracy is the widespread shifting of a state's patrimony into private hands.

Vice President Nguema Obiang Mangue, son of the dictator-president of oil-rich Equatorial Guinea and a seasoned kleptocrat, flew to Brazil on a private plane in late 2018 for medical treatment; Brazilian police and customs officials confiscated large amounts of cash (more than $1.5 million) and handfuls of monogrammed watches worth $15 million. Earlier Nguema Obiang had forfeited cash, automobiles, Michael Jackson memorabilia, and a $30 million mansion in Malibu, California, to escape imprisonment in a US Department of Justice action under its "Kleptocracy Initiative." A French court also convicted Nguema Obiang of embezzlement and seized almost $100 million worth of assets (apartments, cars, and high-end art).

When another conspicuous kleptocrat, Rosmah Mansor, the once-bejeweled wife of disgraced Malaysian former prime minister Najib Razak, was arrested in Putrajaya in 2018 by the country's Anti-Corruption Commission for her part in bilking the state investment fund of at least $731 million and probably as much as $4.5 billion, she forfeited 27 gold necklaces and bangles, 567 handbags, 423 watches, 14 tiaras, bundles of cash, and a twenty-two-carat pink diamond set into a necklace. The whole collection was valued at about $23 million—monies looted from the fund and laundered in the United States and elsewhere. Mansor was charged with receiving a total of $45 million in bribes and seventeen counts of money laundering. Jho Low, a notorious coconspirator, siphoned from the same state fund $250 million with which to purchase a yacht complete with a helicopter landing pad.

Grand corruption breeds inequality. Therefore it is even more directly antagonistic to a nation's economic, social, and political progress than is petty corruption. And the sums sometimes are huge, as indicated earlier. Grand corruption misdirects national policy, substituting projects that benefit individual leaders or small groups of associates for those squarely in the public interest. Much of the proceeds from Zimbabwe's diamond mines, for instance, went to President Robert Mugabe, his wife Grace, and Emmerson Mnangagwa, his presidential successor.

In 2018, Malaysia canceled three large infrastructural projects, including a port and long railway, because its new government suspected that those vast projects were too costly and dependent on long-term financing from China. But the incoming administration also presumed that the projects had only been invented to provide rents for persons close to the administration of former prime minister Razak. Years ago, in Malawi, the president and his wife several times rebuilt a large interior spiral staircase in the new statehouse just so they could extract rents or bribes from foreign construction bidders. In 2019, a memorial hall in a town in KwaZulu-Natal, South Africa, was still undergoing construction after six years of desultory efforts and the expenditure of more than $2 million; local African National Congress officials were killed by other African National Congress militants in a battle to reap the corrupt benefits of the hall's perpetual construction and reconstruction.

Instances of grand corruption are common in nearly all developing countries. But an indictment of Zambia in late 2018 by the *Economist* could stand in for comments on nearly all fragile states where grand corruption rules: the real reason why Zambia had run up debts equal to 59 percent of GDP from 2005 to 2018 was not because of a fall in the price of copper, Zambia's main export commodity, but rather because the nation-state was "run by an inept and venal elite who used easy credit to line their own pockets. Much of the money Zambia borrowed was squandered or stolen. Bigwigs skimmed from worthy-sounding contracts. When the country brought bright new fire engines their price somehow ballooned by 70%, to more than $1 million each. Its new roads mysteriously cost twice as much per kilometer as its neighbours'. Its airport terminal was designed to accommodate an improbable ten-fold jump in traffic. A slide into authoritarianism made corruption harder to check."[16]

But the granddaddy of all grand corruption schemes began in a Brazilian gas station's car wash (Lava Jato), where illegal foreign currency transactions led prosecutors to a huge fraudulent scheme costing Brazil billions of dollars. Directors of Petrobras, the massive national petroleum extracting and producing company, connived with Odebrecht, one of the largest construction companies in South America, to receive payments in exchange for lucrative contracts to build offshore drilling platforms and onshore facilities and housing. Odebrecht overinvoiced so as to receive funds that were "kickbacked" to the directors of Petrobras. They in turn shared their 10 percent or so of every contract with the politicians and political parties that had appointed them to their lucrative positions in the state corporation. Presidents, prime ministers, cabinet officials, and regular parliamentarians were all beneficiaries of this long-running scheme before it was uncovered in 2014, and prosecuted from 2015 through 2018, with many convictions. Meanwhile, the people of Brazil experienced a serious three-year-long recession.

Judge Sérgio Moro, who tried most of the Lava Jato cases, explained that "the focus and concerns of executives at Petrobras were not on the welfare of the company but on opportunities to take bribes, not only for them, but for the politicians who gave them their political support so they could remain in their positions." Moro (later Brazil's minister of justice) added, "The great problem with systemic corruption is not only about economy, about costs," noting that "the major problem is that it affects confidence. For any nation to work, you need confidence in the government, you need confidence in the markets, and you need confidence in democracy. In an environment of systemic corruption, if you add impunity—and impunity was the rule in Brazil before 2014 with some exceptions, of course—you have a lack of confidence in democracy and in the markets, and in the rule of law."[17]

Less conspicuous siphoning of state funds took place in Zimbabwe in 2001 when President Mugabe awarded the nation's largest contract to his nephew for the construction of a modern international airport. In South Africa, frigates and aircraft were purchased from France and Sweden so that leaders of the ruling African National Congress, particularly President Jacob Zuma, could take a healthy cut. Burundi, one of the globe's poorest polities, was pillaged by a president who demanded cash for all cabinet and bureaucratic appointments, and benefited personally from every official construction contract. Tanzanian cabinet ministers found a way in 2014 and 2015 to take large amounts of cash out of the national electricity monopoly's reserve fund and deposit the proceeds in private accounts overseas. The daughter of a recent ruler of Uzbekistan once controlled the government's cell phone licensing arrangements (with large kickbacks) along with several ritzy restaurants, nightclubs, prostitution rings, and trafficking in women. She participated in the "capturing" and criminalizing of Uzbekistan ("criminalized" states will be discussed in chapter 6).

The resource curse is also fundamental to grand corruption. Where there is oil and gas, and sometimes diamonds or even copper, cobalt, and iron ore, and where there is money flowing from wealthy corporations in the North to projects in the South, politicians at the apex of their societies can allocate concessions and permits to favored producers, and reap the proceeds personally (rather than the funds going to the state). In Africa, this has happened in Angola, Chad, the Republic of Congo, the Democratic Republic of Congo, Equatorial Guinea, Gabon, Nigeria, South Sudan, Sudan, and Zimbabwe—all bankrolled by US, European, Brazilian, and now Chinese and Russian concerns.

Abundant opportunities exist in every developing and even some developed countries for those who are politically or bureaucratically in charge to abuse their public positions for vast private gain. Avarice never stops at the edge of a presidential palace or a prime ministerial residence. But it is the indulgences of those at the top of the governing pyramid that sanction the grasping of others lower down the totem pole of corruption. The whole nation consequently makes corruption a way of life. That process saps the nation's resources, diverts tax and royalty payments from national to private purses, and once again robs ordinary citizens of, say, school textbooks and safe cities.

MEASURING AND CONCEPTUALIZING CORRUPTION

For a number of practical policy purposes, and to help make corporate investment and donor foreign assistance decisions, knowing which jurisdictions are less or more corrupt than others is helpful information, and potentially important. Likewise, distinguishing between and among highly corrupt and less corrupt nation-states as finely and as thoroughly as possible can help strengthen reform efforts promoted by civil society or newly elected leaders from within countries, or well-intentioned international organizations from without. Ascertaining which global polities (or even provinces and municipalities) are becoming less or more corrupt over time is also policy relevant, especially if the mechanisms of world order and national governments seek to boost economic development, alleviate poverty, improve health and educational outcomes, and generally uplift standards of living worldwide. Increasing levels of corruption are indicators conducive to the spread of terror, the smuggling of narcotics and people (and sometimes guns), and impending civil conflict.

For all of those good reasons, it is important to disaggregate the striking numbers listed in the previous chapter. Bribes may total a trillion dollars a year, but who is bribing the most, and where are bribes more prevalent and costly? Which nation-states are more prosperous per capita because they have eliminated nearly all propensities to corruption, which are evolving in that direction, and which ones are either falling backward (like Venezuela) or remaining steadily mired in their corrupted morass (like Iran, Nigeria, and Pakistan)? In order to answer such questions in the absence of something objectively measurable, policy makers and opinion shapers need the best-derived kinds of data on a country-by-country basis.

That is hard to obtain. Since corruption is a pervasive way of life in so many countries across the globe, since so many millions and even billions of people are affected daily by the impress of corruption, and since being compelled to offer a bribe or being the unwitting accomplice of a corrupt act is so prevalent, it would seem that it should be easy to record and then to count the actual amounts of cash diverted from proper pursuits to illicit ones. Similarly, the number of corruption-related events—extorted payments, proffered inducements to surly bureaucrats, and kickbacks from contractors to politicians—should be quantifiable. But none of these occurrences is easily witnessed. As Transparency International says officially, "Corruption generally comprises illegal activities which are deliberately hidden and only come to light through scandals, investigations or prosecutions. There is no meaningful way," it concludes, "to assess absolute levels of corruption in countries and territories on the basis of hard empirical data."[1]

What we can do theoretically to compensate is to count up the numbers of bribes reported, prosecutions brought for corruption-related activities, court cases that involve corrupt dealings, and so on. But those instances can hardly be definitive as they mostly show how diligent or not prosecutors and investigators have been, what the media chooses to report or focus on, and—most significantly—what malfeasance has come to light because of accidental or inadvertent exposure. Even if every webcam everywhere managed to videotape every illicit transaction between a police officer and a motorist (theoretically possible, but not yet likely or practical), we still might not be able to capture the full extent of even that category of graft because those who extort bribes would find additional underhanded ways to threaten those on whom they so readily prey.

It is extremely difficult, under the best of circumstances, to gather empirical evidence—necessary and helpful as it would be—of bribe solicitation and delivery, of favors exchanged immediately or promised for some future occasion, and of threats that approximate extortion, especially if little is said explicitly, and because so much of it is episodic rather than systematic. Uncovering contract fraud is possible with careful forensic accounting or the employment of algorithms that sift swiftly through large caches of data, but the number of procurements to be screened makes doing so difficult and expensive. It is also hard to be sure of the number of jobs obtained or appointments accepted without merit, and because of some special "consideration" or promised payments. Keeping track of instances of nepotism is at least cumbersome, if not impossible.

Few receivers of corrupt benefits keep careful accounts (or any accounts at all). After all, because the giving or taking of bribes and favors, the accepting of gifts to do a client "a favor," and the stealing of large or small sums from the public are all serious offenses in every jurisdiction across the globe, these detailed data are bound to remain scarce. Moreover, the consummation of an act of corruption (of whatever kind) is rarely acknowledged on paper or digitally; there are few records, and the actual transactional moments are fleeting. (Note how Governor Robert McDonnell of Virginia was convicted in 2016 of influence peddling by a lower US court and then an appeals court, but subsequently was acquitted by the US

It is extremely difficult, under the best of circumstances, to gather empirical evidence— necessary and helpful as it would be—of bribe solicitation and delivery.

Supreme Court because there were no supposedly tangible benefits provided by the governor to his wealthy patron.) No one has yet managed effectively to gather together and enumerate the myriad guises of corruption—the shadowy manipulations that keep corrupters in business and in thrall.

For all of these perfectly sensible reasons, no accurate way exists as yet to assess the absolute levels of corruption nation by nation or city by city on the basis of hard empirical data. Several ingenious research teams have, however, explored the use of proxy data that enable them to infer how much extra has gone into the construction of bridges or roads, say, above the likely real cost of projects in a given country. In Italy, for example, inventive researchers compared the total public investment in each region with each region's total existing inventory of constructed projects. They were able to find the number and costs of bridges, say, that were "missing"—that would have been erected absent presumed corruption. In one state in Brazil, a researcher along with prosecutorial teams have pioneered a method of finding those construction contracts that appear, at first glance, to be costing more than they should and thus are candidates for further investigation of corruption (see chapter 7). But catching up with corrupt acts and personnel is still no simple task, and the quantification of corrupt dealings within polities or across the planet must also remain a noble work mostly in progress.

As a result, those interested in assessing the true levels of corruption in and across countries and regions are compelled to rely on more subjective than objective data: public surveys, the opinions of so-called experts, the impressions of bankers, journalists, and diplomats with in-country experience, and compilations of anecdotal information. The flaws in these approximating methods are obvious: definitions of corruption may vary from place to place and informant to informant. Selection bias is an obvious peril. Nevertheless, because devising incontrovertible objective measures of corruption that capture its full extent everywhere is a work of the future, we end up depending on measurements across or within countries of (mostly) carefully arranged and controlled "perceptions" of the degree of corrupt behavior.

Indexes of Corruption

For more than two decades, we have relied on two similar subjective indexes of corruption with global reach for our measurements of comparative corruption. Now there are additional indexes with comparable methodologies, and many more that focus on subsets of corrupt behavior. Each employs a number of complementary ways of developing a corruption score for each of the nation-states of the world based on how different sets of observers "perceive" corruption in a particular country. Canada, for example, scores slightly lower (that is, has been perceived as better and less corrupt) than the United States on the two major indexes, and has done so for years. A newer index, using a marginally different methodology, flips the rankings of the neighboring North American countries, again based on somewhat more specialized but still opinion-shaped criteria.

The indexes discussed in what follows are all based on individual opinions gathered annually. None is able to control for the manner in which built-in attitudes or prejudices may influence responses. Urban residents may perceive corruption differently than rural dwellers, and unemployed youths may offer survey answers that are distinct from more settled elders. Nonetheless, aggregating the perceptions of supposedly well-placed experts, businesspeople, and opinion shapers about the extent of public sector corruption or corporate venality remains the most common, and possibly the most effective, method of comparing levels of corruption across nations or other political jurisdictions. Despite legitimate questions about whether external perceptions, no matter how scientifically gathered, approximate actual experience, the existing indexes constitute the gold standard. They offer the most widely accepted way of approximating corrupt activity across the globe.

The best-known and most widely used measures of corruption are Transparency International's Corruption Perceptions Index (CPI) and the World Bank Institute's Control of Corruption Indicator (CCI). (Transparency International, a well-regarded nongovernmental organization [NGO] based in Berlin, Germany, has battled corruption since 1993. The World Bank Institute is a part of the World Bank, located in Washington, DC.) The first measure was begun in 1995, and the second in 1996. In 2019, the first rated 180 countries, and the second rated 215. The CPI ranks countries and territories by their perceived levels of public sector corruption. The CCI officially "captures perceptions of the extent to which public power is exercised for private gain."

Their methodologies are essentially the same. The CPI is derived each year from opinions gathered initially by and filtered through twelve institutions and subindex sources, such as the African Development Bank Governance Ratings, the Bertelsmann Foundation Transformation Index, the Economist Intelligence Unit Country Risk Ratings, Freedom House's Nations in Transit, several commercial risk assessment compilations, and the World Economic Forum's Executive Opinion Survey. The CCI in turn comes from thirty-two indicators and surveys that capture the experiences of "citizens, entrepreneurs, and experts." It depends for its inputs on nine surveys of households and firms, results from four commercial business information providers, eleven reports from NGOs such as Freedom House, and eight data sets produced by the World Bank. But it also sends influential questionnaires to the Bertelsmann Foundation, the International Budget Survey, regional development banks, and many additional organizations. The list of sources on which the CCI is based is much longer than the CPI's, but includes an overlapping ten or so institutions.

The makers of both indexes rely on their sources for digests of opinions from persons who are truly "expert." These received perceptions are turned into numerical scores, standardized, and ultimately computed and published as simple averages. That process seems straightforward and is easily justified. But more or less corruption may not mean the same thing to the so-called experts, and "corruption" is not defined strictly. Moreover, not all of the providers answer the same questions; some of the respondents are based in the countries being rated, and some are not; some opinions come from massaged group discussions in a supplying organization like the African Development Bank; and some of the ratings supplied to the CPI and CCI are out-of-date when issued, based on data compiled for other purposes and projects. Furthermore, it is somewhat telling that the rankings of countries in both the major indexes have not changed significantly over more than two decades. Ninety percent of the current ratings in both indexes are explained by ratings a decade or more before.

Despite those and other criticisms of the premier corruption measuring tools, our judgment of a nation-state's level of corruption is largely, and almost exclusively, derived from scores provided annually by the CPI and CCI. Without too much exception, when their respective rankings are released each year in Berlin or Washington, DC, the countries at the top—the countries that are judged least corrupt—and those at the bottom—the most rampantly corrupt—are much the same, although sometimes in a slightly different order than the year before.

The Nordic nations and New Zealand are always at the apex of the list, sometimes with Finland in the lead, sometimes Denmark, and occasionally New Zealand. The top ten least corrupt countries always include the Nordic nations, New Zealand, Iceland, Singapore, and Canada. Sometimes Germany, the United Kingdom, the Netherlands, or Luxembourg, and occasionally Switzerland, join the elite dozen or so. The United States is always in the next decile, along with France. Uruguay ranks best in South America, and Botswana and the Seychelles in Africa. At the bottom of both listings we can count on Somalia, North Korea, Venezuela, Iraq, Libya, Angola, South Sudan, the Sudan, Afghanistan, Nigeria, Chad, and Zimbabwe. Occasionally, there is movement within the middle ranks. Argentina's standing improved under the Macri government; the Lava Jato scandal caused Brazil's ranking to fall substantially.

The Index of Public Integrity, established by a research team housed at the Hertie School of Politics, also in Berlin, rates 120 countries. It attempts to measure corruption somewhat more objectively than the CPI and the CCI. It was first introduced in 2016 and is produced annually. Its ranks are developed from six closely related components "associated with control of corruption": judicial independence, administrative burden (based on the World Bank's Doing Business Data), trade openness, budget transparency, e-citizenship (based on the percentages of the population that have broadband access and use Facebook), and press freedom. Several but not all of these variables depend on expert opinion polls, just like the CPI and CCI. Judicial independence is based on an expert opinion survey, as is the budget openness question and press freedom. Overall, because the other categories of analysis use less subjective inputs, the Index of Public Integrity provides a measurement system that is more objective and possibly more accurate than its predecessors. Its initial results, however, correlated closely to the findings of the CPI and the CCI. The Nordic nations were highly rated along with New Zealand, the Netherlands, the United Kingdom, Ireland, and Luxembourg. The United States ranked highly, however, and did even better than Estonia and Germany. At the bottom of the scale (with fewer countries in total) were the usual suspects: Venezuela, Chad, Myanmar, Cambodia, Zimbabwe, Tajikistan, Bolivia, and Nepal.

Those are three measuring devices. Also helpful in differentiating countries globally is the World Justice Project's Rule of Law Index, again based on the views of in-country experts but with the added input of numbers of citizens in most of the polities covered. (The World Justice Project, in Washington, DC, is an independent NGO created to strengthen the rule of law globally.) The index includes an "absence of corruption" indicator that is constructed from answers by "qualified respondents" to sixty-eight questions, most of which are carefully constructed to elicit responses helpful in scoring the globe's constituents. This index covers 113 countries.

For cross-country comparable analysis, researchers and opinion makers can also consult the Bribe Payers Index (a listing of the main exporters of corrupt inducements), the World Bank Business Environment Survey (which asks business executives how much they pay out in bribes to public officials overseas), the World Bank Institutional Integrity blacklists (which cite companies for corrupt dealings and prevent them from bidding on World Bank–sponsored contracts), and the Global Corruption Barometer (which is used in particular countries to ascertain from citizen surveys whether corruption is increasing and what percentages of citizens pay bribes). In its last iteration, the barometer obtained responses from 114,000 persons in 107 countries. Sierra Leone, Liberia, Yemen, and Kenya reported the most corruption; Australia, Denmark, Finland, and Japan the least.

The Financial Secrecy Index shows how fully open or closed companies are, and how efficiently countries collect taxes—both of which are relevant issues for corruption. With greater transparency, corruption is less common and easier to discern. When taxes are hard to collect because of opaque and obscure financial proceedings and covert markets, corruption can flourish.

An Anti–Money Laundering Index covers 152 countries, reporting on how well countries regulate and police this correlate to corruption. The Open Budget Survey and Index discloses the availability of key budget documents and information from 102 nations, and rates them accordingly. The ID Search, a project of the Organized Crime and Corruption Reporting Project (responsible for the Panama Papers), contains millions of documents derived from company records, court cases, leaks of information, and more.

The *Economist* has compiled a crony capitalism index to see whether "robber barons"—kleptocrats—are growing more powerful. Russia, Malaysia, and the Philippines have the largest percentages of billionaire wealth to GDP globally. The Resource Governance Index evaluates the extent to which 58 nations with substantial oil, gas, and mineral riches (frequently sources of rents and corruption) are transparent and accountable. The EITI and Extractive Fisheries Transparency Initiative admit countries to their august ranks if they disclose all of their revenues from the multinational corporations that hold or obtain mining or other exploitative resource concessions. The Maritime Anti-Corruption Network tries to accomplish similar objectives for the shipping industry.

In order to begin to curb corruption, reliable knowledge about where it abounds and where it has been reduced is essential. That information enables us to advocate for and experiment with the kinds of reforms that could help to reduce corrupt practices and strengthen any anticorruption initiatives. Without these varied data it would be difficult to demonstrate which kinds of initiatives have been employed positively and which ones have been difficult to sustain. Evidence-based endeavors are impossible without the existing estimates of corruption's intensity.

The existence of the indexes, especially the well-regarded ones, keeps the spotlight on corruption within countries. By itself, the indexing procedure maintains pressure on corruption as a global malaise. Outcomes in individual countries are also made available so that civil societies, ruling regimes, donors, and world powers can all battle corruption strenuously and successfully.

Even more critically, the struggle against corruption in all of its guises fundamentally depends on reliable knowledge. What the several indexes and other often-proxy

In order to begin to curb corruption, reliable knowledge about where it abounds and where it has been reduced is essential.

measures of corruption do is to provide "goals to be chased, accountabilities to be improved, [and] transparencies to be perfected."[2] Without the masses of information that the measurement tools offer, governments, civil societies, international organizations, the big global lenders of first resort, national donor agencies, and various watchdog institutions would be far less able to diagnose crucial developmental issues as well as how to ameliorate them. Absent the indexes, knowing exactly where to press hard for anticorruption returns, or to mount initiatives capable of lessening the impact of corruption globally and nationally, would be harder and less certain.

"GETTING TO DENMARK": COMBATING CORRUPTION, THE PATH FORWARD

We know that corruption is capable of being reduced on the national scene, even nearly extirpated, because a number of mostly small, tightly controlled, nation-states have in modern times succeeded in moving from eras of wholesale corruption to the embrace of pursuits almost fully ethical. Three states, two small and one of medium size (Botswana, Singapore, and Rwanda), managed in the late twentieth and early twenty-first centuries to develop successfully by drastically diminishing corruption and by engendering widespread alterations in how their peoples regard matters corrupt. Populous China may also be changing attitudes toward corrupt practices despite President Xi Jinping's anticorruption drive being designed to accomplish other, authoritarian political objectives. In the cases of China, Singapore, and Rwanda, of course, curtailing corruption has also accompanied the curtailing of essential freedoms. But, as the case of Botswana (discussed below) exemplifies, diminishing corruption need not diminish human rights and civil liberties.

Fortunately, to buttress what we have learned from the contemporary experience of those democratic and quasidemocratic entities that have beaten back corruption and effectively altered their prevailing political cultures, we also now understand that today's least corrupt countries were once themselves promiscuously crooked, but thanks to gifted leadership, the influence of the Enlightenment, the spread of mass education, the emergence of national churches, and the rise of merit-based bureaucratic systems, they shifted incrementally over many nineteenth- and early twentieth-century decades from widespread to limited tolerance of corruption. In other words, what took place over centuries in Europe's north and in the antipodes could—difficult as it appears—someday soon take place in the numerous countries where corruption currently flourishes.

Shifting the people of a nation or some smaller political entity from enduring corruption as an annoying and costly but inevitable way of life to the outright rejection and refusal to participate in corrupt activities is the only proven method of reducing corruption globally. The small states of Hong Kong and Singapore did so in the 1970s and 1980s, almost overnight, and transformed what had been wide open and wildly corrupt cities largely controlled by or benefiting Chinese triads (gangs) and British police officers into today's mostly pristine polities. Under the authoritarian rule of President Paul Kagame, Rwanda has done the same, and with equal speed. In democratic Botswana, its first president adamantly opposed corruption of any kind and enduringly banished it from his newly independent African state in 1966.

These modern examples of corruption's retreat unwittingly emulate the major attitudinal shifts that took place far less swiftly, but sustainably, first in eighteenth- and early nineteenth-century Denmark, then elsewhere in the Nordic nations, Prussia, the Netherlands, and eventually New Zealand, the United Kingdom, and Canada. The United States, with a woefully corrupt national government until at least 1881, followed this trend under the leadership of President Chester Arthur. But it took several more decades before corruption levels fell, and Tammany Hall along with other municipal and state corruption rings were fully exposed and tamed, in part by the actions of New York City's police commissioner and later President Theodore Roosevelt.

Public attitudes altered. Otherwise there would have been little significant change, hardly any progress, and only a limited lessening of the corrupt pursuits that had captured innumerable US city and town halls. What had happened over considerable time in the successful societal rejections of corruption in Europe and elsewhere was not that improved morals and enhanced ethical behavior had permeated these jurisdictions. Nor had ramped up punishment done the deed. Instead, as in the modern cases and some of the older international examples, a leader or a set of new leaders had helped whole societies to reject corruption, and to emphasize the long-term importance to them as individuals and to society of integrity in public and private life. Comprehensive visions of fairness replaced corrupted business as usual.

Collective Behavior

The secret to creating corruption- and largely graft-free nation-states is to substitute new behavioral patterns for older ones, and to do so by (forcibly or gently) acculturating citizens to regard participating in acts of corruption, of whatever kind, as shameful. Yes, the fear of getting caught and punished is always helpful. The possibility of prison wonderfully concentrates the mind. But the key to reducing the propensity to corrupt and be corrupted down to near nothing can only be achieved by changing collective behavior. That is what the Nordic nations, New Zealand, and Canada began to do in the nineteenth century, and perfected well into the twentieth century. That is what is being accomplished much more rapidly today in Rwanda, Estonia, and Croatia.

Change agents like Kagame and Prime Minister Lee of Singapore intuitively understood what scholars now also accept: corruption must be fixed by disrupting collective behavior, not simply by forcibly banning actions and actors that are corrupt and corrupting. We need no longer conceptualize corruption as a principal-agent problem where the agent—the low-level bureaucrat behind the grille, the permitting authority, the police officer at a roadblock, or the judge sitting on a decision—betrays her benevolent principal, the king in olden times, and the public interest and high-level political leaders today. Now we know that reducing corruption is much more than removing bad agents or regulating their actions so that they observe their obligations to the public interest (and the king) more strictly. Similarly, curbing corruption depends on much more than removing corruption-inducing incentives (although doing so is bound to help), reducing the discretionary ambit of agents, and putting agents under full-time scrutiny. What is essential, we have learned over decades, is that corrupt practices persist until there is a wholesale societal reorientation initiated by committed leadership (much more than a principal agent), or developed across and within a national body politic.

All kinds of corruption become embedded in society when it is common and expected, and when it becomes the default amoral norm. Disengaging from corrupt practice thus becomes difficult since refusing bribes and

What is essential, we have learned over decades, is that corrupt practices persist until there is a wholesale societal reorientation initiated by committed leadership, or developed across and within a national body politic.

kickbacks, and refraining from using one's position of authority within, say, a developing economy, is irrational. "Public officials," researchers conclude, "who refuse to take advantage of their positions to enrich themselves are regarded [by friends and relatives] as stupid and may even face ridicule."[1]

Moreover, kleptocracy is caused by acquisitiveness by rogue political powers acting as principals. In nearly all cases globally, the culpability of agents is less the problem than it is the malevolence of principals. Most grand and even petty corruption emanates from the top. A president, prime minister, ruling military officer, governor, or mayor shows the way by demanding a percentage of contracts and concessions for him or herself and his or her cronies, grabbing rents from each barrel of oil or ton of iron ore exported from her or his polity, and then permitting underlings to do the same. Just like a fish rots from the head, so corruption of every kind takes its shape and direction from a high-level principal among principals.

Too many kleptocrats and their ilk self-define the public interest as the interests of themselves, their families, and their associates. As self-interest rather than national interest maximizers, they think that it is their turn "to eat." Thus the principals must be reformed as well as their agents. This shift comes about most readily when the societal collective rises up to demand more transparency and accountability, or when rogue principals finally understand themselves that corruption is inefficient and unacceptable, and indeed that it is shameful. Coups d'état sometimes create such receptivity to change, as in the Sudan. Sometimes elections do so too, as in Malaysia in 2018. But the hardest-to-generate societal shifts are also the most salutary and sustainable—the transformation of fundamental societal norms or whole political cultures to regard (at last) the pursuit of corrupt gains as personally and collectively abhorrent and aberrant. That behavioral transformation took place in Denmark at the end of the eighteenth century and extended well into the nineteenth century, stimulated by monarchical preferences, and nurtured by improved schooling and a number of other changes within Scandinavian life. It also happened in modern Botswana when political leaders showed that integrity worked and that corruption was harmful.

Reducing the scourge of corruption always requires long-term efforts on the parts of leaders, electorates, independent judges, and legislators to persuade citizens that the state (or the province) will serve them best if it is not lubricated—if position and influence are not purchased and merit prevails. Agents are less the problem than the prevailing ethos within which they serve. So the ethos must be changed, and that is best done from the political apex of a nation or some other comparable political jurisdiction.

More democracy is not necessarily the answer. Nor are stronger or better institutions on their own, although they can help if they are rebuilt as a result of citizen protests. Conceivably, the mere supply of more democracy might be salutary in reducing the amount of corruption in a country, but the available research shows instead that improved governance, stronger rules of law, and decisive accountability matter more than, say, free and fair elections.

Although democracy is much more prevalent globally than it was fifty or forty years ago, especially in Africa, there is no less corruption. In fact, more democracy (however defined and construed) need not mean less corruption. Zimbabwe's return to nominal democracy after an election in 2018 has not meant any mitigation of corruption. Nor, across the universe of fragile states, does economic growth per capita and rising incomes remove the temptation of corruption. Sometimes democracy (or electoral democracy) even enables corrupt practices, as in most of the oil-rich states.

Ethical Universalism

The answer, overall, is a turn toward ethical universalism or, at a minimum, the calculated decisions of strong leaders (like Kagame and Lee) who impose their will on corrupt societies or (like Sir Seretse Khama of Botswana) can gradually move their followers away from the lure of corruption. Only farsighted transformational leaders (as I discuss in chapter 8) can break out of the collective social trap of corruption. Only persuasive leadership can dismantle that trap, or destroy it and guide their voters or followers to regard the public interest as a collective good. In other words, the task of leadership is to demonstrate why and how corruption is no longer efficacious or acceptable as a collective pursuit. And that means leading citizens toward an embrace of what we call ethical universalism.

Ethical universalism presumes that all inhabitants of a political jurisdiction will be treated fairly, equally, and tolerantly. At its best, that means that within a political and policy framework of ethical universalism, minorities are treated as well, with the same privileges and opportunities, as majorities, and that religious, racial, and other identities gain rights the same way as any other group or person within a political space. The antithesis of ethical universalism is particularism, the current disposition of so many of the world's underprivileged citizens. Particularism regards individuals and groups differentially, depending on their (supposedly inferior) characteristics. Particularism enables and motivates corruption. They go hand in hand.

Ethical universalism exists as a collective good. In countries such as New Zealand and Sweden, for example, the transition from accepting to forbidding corruption took place over centuries. Likewise, the broad acceptance of ethical universalism as a central component of national political cultures took a long time. But as an awareness of the importance of ethical universalism grew, first in northern Europe, so did the societal embrace of the significance of public and personal integrity, buttressed rules of law, and formal and informal intolerance of acts that could be construed as corrupt, and therefore against an emerging sense of the public interest. So also grew the demand for judicial independence and court judgments free of partiality or undue influence. All of this gradual adherence to ethical universalism came with increased civic participation and, especially, more citizen demands for better performance from public servants of all kinds.

In the modern era, in places such as Hong Kong and Singapore, the shift from particularism to ethical universalism has come about much more abruptly, in accelerated time. Corrupt actors were prosecuted and punished, of course, but the leaders of those places and others emphasized how collectively harmful and socially disruptive corrupt pursuits were, and how continued corruption would constitute a drag on national prosperity, on developmental goals, and on moving from third world to first world status. Those jurisdictions, especially Hong Kong, focused on educating their citizens to reject all forms of corrupt behavior (see chapter 5). In a matter of decades, a new sense of ethical universalism pervaded those city-states as well as countries like Botswana.

By preaching ethical universalism, and practicing it, these modern states, like the earlier Nordic and antipodean examples, gained legitimacy as rampant practices of corruption receded into the past. The shift to ethical universalism instead of particularism and corruption accompanies rises in social trust, increased transparency, and an underlining of the importance of public service in the public interest. As the originator of the concept concludes, "Ethical universalism becomes an institution [and an emerging norm] ... rather than a mere ideology ... when a significant part of society share[s] the belief in the superiority of ethical universalism over particularism."[2]

To reemphasize, the broad socialization of the norm of ethical universalism is the ultimate goal of all anticorruption efforts. At its fullest, it champions the reconfiguring of societal modes of behavior. Shifting the expectations of ruling elites is key, as is stressing a new ethic of public service. A new political culture is created and extended. Old ways of doing business are discarded.

The Nordic Experiments

"If only everyone could be like the Scandinavians," extolled President Barack Obama, beating back corruption "would all be easy."[3] He and I do not mean that corruption is completely banished in the far north of Europe; rather, political culture and societal norms in those places abhor corrupt dealings so much that being accused of any form of corruption is shameful and embarrassing, as well as criminal. Visitors to such places do not expect routinely to be asked for a bribe or to hand over brown envelopes filled with cash to obtain better service. It is not that the Swedes, Danes, and others like them are better persons, or that there is something in their DNA that makes them now eschew corruption. Instead, it is the fact that the top dozen or so performers on the CPI have citizenries and national political cultures that have adopted ethical universalism as their core calling. That means that they exhibit high levels of social trust, are wealthy with low levels of inequality, are well educated, and expect integrity and openness from their politicians and civil servants.

But it was not always thus, and that is why the story of the Nordics, the Prussians, the antipodean outposts, and other countries such as Canada is so instructive in fashioning successful anticorruption efforts in the twenty-first century.

Denmark was the first to inaugurate the shift from corrupt rule to new forms of governance that more and more, over at least two centuries, were noncorrupt in their essence. Kings were still selling state offices and tax-collecting opportunities during the early eighteenth century, but toward the end of that century Danish kings had begun to rely less for the administration of their realm on a decentralized, greedy, aristocracy, and more readily on a new cadre of civil servants paid for by and loyal to the monarchy. Successive kings, with parallel developments in Sweden, demanded professionalism and honest tax collecting; during the late eighteenth century they even introduced a meritocracy of bourgeois bureaucrats policed by prosecutors who could ferret out abuses of office. Later, in the early nineteenth century, judges were required to be graduates of the University of Copenhagen. That turn toward graduates and professionals in the northern outposts of Europe helped to guide Denmark and Sweden, and later Norway, Iceland, and Finland (all controlled at that time by either Denmark or Sweden), toward the promised land of probity, based on the observance of the rule of law (and against tendencies to corrupt).

Another major contribution to these attitudinal shifts took place in Denmark in the late eighteenth century, when kings sought greater legitimacy and the backing of their subjects; they opened their ears to citizen voices and, specifically, started to receive petitions of complaint—as many as twelve thousand annually by the end of the century. Public opinion began to be heard and then to have an impact on public policy. This openness increased social trust, made the rule of kings seem less arbitrary, and helped to move Denmark and its people to take stands against anything that smacked of corruption. After the Napoleonic wars, citizen complaints about corruption, and how corruption affected their daily lives, led to a newly rigorous oversight of functionaries and to audits of official books everywhere.

All of these incremental events were intended to reassure citizens and boost the legitimacy of the Danish monarchy. New laws against corruption were passed, further strengthening an emerging anticorruption norm. By the mid-nineteenth century, too, a new penal code provided specific penalties for corruption. Civil servants started to receive fixed salaries and pensions, and corrupt activity began to recede.

In about the mid-nineteenth century as well, Danes had shifted from thinking of themselves as belonging to "an estate," as they had been accustomed to doing earlier. They began to think of themselves as a people. Danes started to identify with the state, and especially with a state that had begun behaving in an ethically universalist manner. Danish, the vernacular, became the language of the court and business. Schooling became universal and free from 1814, shifting to Danish from German and Latin throughout the first half of the century. The state Lutheran Church also became more democratic, and the growth of folk and more individualistic forms of Protestantism all contributed to an emerging Danish identity as well as to a pronounced opposition to corruption. Social cohesion grew as citizens became more literate and as they started, with the acquiescence of the crown, to gain more control over all parts of their lives. They were ethically universalist in a fundamental sense even before they enjoyed democracy (after 1849) and in an era when anticorruption had become an emerging civic norm.

Sweden's twenty-first century disdain for corruption has many of the same roots as Denmark, and since either or both ruled for much of the nineteenth century over Norway and Iceland, and Finland (until 1809), Swedish and Danish tutelage helps to explain why the Nordic nations moved together so dramatically from their early corrupt pursuits to what we now call ethical universalism.

The Swedes enjoyed a liberal constitution (for the period) in the early eighteenth century but then were ruled by a rather absolutist king, supported by the military, from 1771 to 1792. His successors in the Napoleonic era had the misfortune to lose a major war against Russia (and forfeit Finland) and to battle Denmark on the country's southern flank. Dissatisfied military officers staged a coup d'état to remove King Gustavus IV Adolphus, write a liberal new constitution, and install a French field marshal and compatriot of Napoléon as their new monarch and leader.

These major experiments in governance led to a much more people-centered parliamentary control of policy than ever before, to increased judicial power, to a rash of new laws and procedures to enforce honest dealings in the rural areas, and to a ban on the purchase of military, clerical, and secular positions of prominence. Meritocratic promotions after examinations became the norm, as earlier in Denmark. By 1834, according to an analysis of debates in the Riksdag (Parliament), there was agreement that public servants owed their loyalty and best endeavors to the nation, not to themselves or their patrons, and that impartiality was expected.

Sweden, under its French monarch, and in keeping with the spirit of the European Age of Enlightenment, was protected against chicanery from within by incipient Swedish democrats, industrialists, less conservative nobles, and forward-looking representatives of the peasant estate. Sweden's press was free, too, by the standards of the time and active in criticizing questionable political developments. Sweden's universities were also growing in quality during the nineteenth century and beginning to supply a new generation of civil servants. Possibly most important of all, Sweden was greatly expanding its free primary and secondary educational system, and enabling a great rise in literacy. Swedes were simultaneously forging a Swedish identity that was new.

Civil society was expanding as well. Sweden experienced a great rise in voluntary associations, temperance pressure groups, church and bible study bodies, poorhouses and relief efforts for the impoverished, labor unions, and professional organizations with middle-class origins.

An old view that holders of administrative positions could serve themselves was discarded. By 1862, the Riksdag in Sweden legislated strong sanctions for official "misconduct" by bureaucrats. A half century later, all these forces produced within Sweden and Norway (which it ruled) a decided, enduring, public opposition to corruption.

Political will and determined leadership helped in Denmark and Sweden, and therefore in the other Nordic lands, to delegitimize corruption from the nineteenth century onward. Strongly principled monarchs imposed high service standards and introduced rules against theft by their civil servants. People's willingness to pay taxes and supply soldiers (for wars and upgrading social standards) was enhanced by the integrity of their kings and the integrity of the kingly enterprise (an attribute important to the success of Botswana and Singapore as well).

All of these factors and others gradually produced a profound intolerance of corruption—of all manner of personally enriching escapades that detracted from the emerging ethic of public service. Accountability became fundamental. Anything and everything that detracted in any manner from a well-functioning state and citizen-centered service enterprise was deprecated. The norm of ethical universalism took hold.

In the Antipodes

The transformation of New Zealand and Australia from frontier settlements heavily immersed in corruption to their late twentieth and early twenty-first century statuses as relative paragons of virtue somewhat mimics the Scandinavian transit from self-dealing to public regard. Yet the early occupiers of both distant outposts of Her Majesty's Victorian realm were transplants—in New Zealand's case, carefully selected middle-class, educated, church-attending, mostly Presbyterian family units that were content to be "respectable." Democratic practices arrived with the settlers in the 1840s; the press was free and vibrant from the start.

Two more waves of immigration, first gold miners and then British-assisted indigents, greatly swelled the European-derived population and gave rise to corruption, especially with regard to the taking of land from the indigenous Maori in contravention of the spirit and letter of the Treaty of Waitangi. Prominent appointments to the civil service were dependent on patronage; nepotism was rife in the House of Assembly and the bureaucracy. "Jobbery" (graft) flourished until at least 1912, when the Public Service Act began to alter the ways in which New Zealanders regarded public service.

Egalitarianism, possibly the product of a rough and sparsely populated pioneering atmosphere, was the prevailing sentiment. Individualism and libertarianism were less significant sentiments. By the turn of the twentieth century, too, this preference for equal treatment morphed into a distinctive preference for social justice, ignoring the settler treatment of the Maori. Whites in New Zealand were discouraged from taking undue advantage of each other, especially corruptly. Democratic from the beginning, New Zealand gave the vote to women as early as 1893.

But, in terms of the government becoming noncorrupt, it was more important that the early New Zealand settlers had close ties to the land, relied almost exclusively on sheep and dairy farming, and were homogeneous. Everything was on a small scale, distant from the pulsating industrial cities that they had left behind. These factors, together, fostered abundant social trust and social capital, modesty, probity, and, over time, a partiality to honest dealings. Certainly from the 1920s onward, public servants were devoted to the ideal of honest public service. Fair laws and auditing requirements were put in place to reinforce what had become a national embrace of ethical universalism.

New Zealand has always ranked higher in the perceptions and other indexes of corruption than Australia, its Oceanic neighbor, despite their relatively contemporaneous settlements from Britain. Conceivably, New Zealanders came across the waters more thoroughly imbued with British nineteenth-century egalitarian values than the Australians who were transported to penal colonies. The latter obviously derived from a less lofty social class, but whether or not that made a crucial difference is unclear. The Australians were more Catholic than Protestant, and that could have been decisive. Australia's population in the nineteenth century was more numerous than New Zealand's, and that may also have been a factor. It was not until the 1930s that new leadership articulated and imposed energetic reforms on the Australian civil service. That led, in time, to a diminution of corruption by public servants and politicians.

Canada

Like the premodern Nordics, early Canada, even before the creation of the Canadian confederation in 1867, was rife with patronage. Public servants plundered wherever they could, and gave procurement contracts to favorites prepared to offer substantial kickbacks. Even an early and popular prime minister (Sir John A. Macdonald) was proud to participate, demanding sizable gifts to approve railway concessions and construction applications. Sir Wilfred Laurier, a slightly later prime minister, and his associates all profited from control over the lucrative national fiscal trough. According to one authoritative source, before World War I, Canada abounded in "stuffed envelopes quietly passed on street corners, nervous winks, and even telephone taps."[4] This comparatively open practice of corruption in the provinces as well as in the public works and provincial liquor control realms continued into the 1960s.

By then, however, over many decades and especially at the federal level, Canadians had grown intolerant of such corrupt activity. Politicians and civil servants led by strong-minded leaders conscious that their citizens and constituents had begun to behave as ethical universalists refrained more and more from accepting gifts for favors. Even so, or consequently, Prime Minister Lester Pearson in 1964 felt a responsibility to remind his colleagues and appointees that they had an obligation to act scrupulously. "The conduct of public business," he lectured, "must be beyond question in terms of moral standards."[5]

Becoming Noncorrupt

These sketches, and the many more examples that are available, demonstrate that it was feasible in earlier centuries to move whole nations from the widespread practice of corruption to a highly developed antipathy to such malfeasance and sleaze. The experiences of the Nordic nations, antipodean states, and several other European nations and Canada show that it was possible, over considerable time, to evolve peoples and societies to enshrine ethical universalism, and to shun particularism and corruption. In each case there were leaders who articulated the need to turn national backs on what had been wholesale corruption. Those leaders were sometimes kings, sometimes politicians, frequently newly empowered bureaucrats, and often persons in civil society who influenced at least considerable portions of their societal shifts away from numbly accepting contract fraud and other forms of graft. In each case, too, their societies were modernizing, benefiting from increased literacy, enhanced levels of social trust, and greater awareness of their national identities.

Critical to such a transition is a reframing over time of the national political culture. The provision of new educational opportunity is also critical. Those collective behavioral shifts are more important than the provision of more democracy, stronger rules of law, economic growth, better institutions, and the accumulation of capital.

This chapter shows that corruption is neither inevitable nor immutable. It also demonstrates that the very people who are hopelessly addicted to corrupt rewards can, suitably led and inspired, turn their backs on such pursuits and assimilate new anticorruption initiatives. Modern-day transitions like those of the early Danes or later Canadians are possible, even without the visionary leadership of a Lee or the actions of an autocratic Kagame. But transformative change still needs leadership at critical times and critical levels.

POSITIVE EXAMPLES IN
LATIN AMERICA

Amid the collection of developing world countries and
weak and failed states that are mostly corrupt (according
to the indexes), there are a scattered handful that are less
corrupt, ranking below the Nordic nations, Canada, Australia, and the United States, but well ahead of their peers.
In Latin America, for example, where the sinewy tentacles
of the Lava Jato scandal have implicated Brazil, Bolivia,
Peru, Colombia, Venezuela, Honduras, Guatemala, and
Mexico, among others, and where wholesale corruption
has characterized nearly every nation for decades, Uruguay,
Chile, and Costa Rica alone score highly, and are regarded
as far less corrupted countries than their neighbors and
peers. Why? Why and how did Georgia, almost uniquely
among ex-Soviet states, battle so effectively against corruption? These states, and a few others such as Mauritius

and Cape Verde, join Botswana, the Seychelles, Singapore, Hong Kong, and Rwanda as the least corrupted outliers in their regions. How and why did they resist succumbing to the incubus of corruption?

Uruguayian Exceptionalism

Uruguay emerged from its colonial past with a very different approach than its neighbors regarding the sanctity of the general interest as opposed to favoring personal interest and condoning the abuse of public office. As a collective behavioral approach, its contained population, mostly engaged in agricultural pursuits, frowned on corrupt practices. By 1916, political leaders and the political parties that competed for votes had developed what they called the practice of coparticipation. Power and clientelistic practices were largely rejected at the leadership level. Avoidance of political competition and the sharing of the outcomes of office holding became the norm, guided by early political leaders. The pressure to amass campaign funds—one of the several key drivers of corruption everywhere—was limited since the ultimate stakes, leaders agreed, were rather small. Moreover, in these early years of the Uruguayan republic, its citizens grew wealthier per capita than other South Americans. They were able to pursue improved educational opportunities. Overall, by the mid-twentieth century, Uruguay was a modernization success story.

Uruguay's judges are well respected even if the processing of court cases is slow and cumbersome. The police are regarded as comparatively honest. Only 7 percent (a low number by global standards) of Uruguayans said that they had been asked for a bribe to access public services in 2014. Eighty-three percent of Uruguayans, according to a Latinobarómetro poll in 2015, had not experienced corruption or heard of it in the two months prior to the survey.[1] Moreover, irregular payments or bribes in connection to annual tax payments are uncommon. Procurement issues—kickbacks to secure contracts for public works projects or supplies—are infrequent. International money laundering exists, but in 2019 was being contained and prosecuted. In sum, compared to the rest of Latin America, Uruguay experiences markedly less corruption. Furthermore, when corrupt dealings or questionable conflicts of interests are revealed by investigatory media or other means, political leaders react ethically, and the populace in Uruguay is critical and appropriately appalled. Ethical universalism, in other words, largely prevails.

Uruguay's small population of 3.5 million socially integrated persons may have helped to contribute to its noncorrupt success story. It has fewer people than even Singapore and Hong Kong. The small size and homogeneity of its population, however, may not be conclusive.

Other South American countries are also homogeneous and yet more corrupt.

Whereas those who seek cultural explanations for corruption might want to point to something in Chile's population composition and to the fact that Chile was settled later than other South American countries (as opposed to Spain's early influence on Bolivia, Peru, and Ecuador), its peoples came as much from Spain as other places. Chile does harbor pockets of Basque, Croatian, and German immigration, and some Uruguayans are descended from Italians (as in much of southern Brazil) and the Swiss, but deriving something distinctive from such ethnic and cultural origins cannot explain either Uruguay's or Chile's twenty-first century outcomes.

In seeking explanations for anticorruption attitudes and actions, the kinds of open, democratic, and courageous political leadership that Uruguay has enjoyed since the end of the military dictatorship in 1985 may be decisive. The same outcomes may be important in appreciating why post-Pinochet Chile ranks highly on the indexes. Uruguay (and also Chile and Costa Rica) has transitioned away from military control toward a multiparty system that, in contrast with many of its neighbors and peers, has not depended on shady financing schemes for political campaigns. After 1985, the appeal to voters of programmatic political parties reduced the role of clientelism and helped to lead the country away from particularism to universalism. Nor has Uruguay relied as much as its peers and neighbors on patrimonial appeals for loyalty and support. In terms of patronage, and appointments to the numerous and influential state-owned enterprises, Uruguay's parties still share across party lines much more effectively than do their counterparts elsewhere. That sense of compromise and an ethical universalistic approach, plus the absence of a zero-sum view of public perquisites, contribute to limited competition and reduced corruption. Most of all, the evenhanded decisions made by an array of political leaders have done for Uruguay what a succession of the nineteenth-century compromises did for Denmark and Sweden.

Uruguay is almost completely literate, as are Chile and Costa Rica. As in the Nordic cases during the nineteenth and twentieth centuries, being well educated often militates against any tolerance of corruption. Building on these literary and schooling attainments, Uruguay is blessed with an unusually free and fearless media for Spanish-speaking Latin America—a feature also present in Chile and now in Costa Rica. One small institution unique to Uruguay—the Junta de Transparencia y Ética Pública—manages and monitors asset declarations by public servants and procurement decisions by public sector agencies—something that could easily be done elsewhere, and to good effect. It trains officials and promotes ethics and transparency throughout the government, and

As in the Nordic cases during the nineteenth and twentieth centuries, being well educated often militates against any tolerance of corruption.

has played an important role in maintaining Uruguay's positive reputation since 1998.

Uruguay also has strong laws that hold politicians and officials accountable, but so do Argentina and Chile; impunity has never been conferred or expected in Uruguay, Chile, and Costa Rica since their military eras. Other contested polities do not yet enjoy such a legal bedrock.

Chile after Military Dictatorship

Explanations for Chile's comparatively limited levels of "low-intensity" corruption also, along with Uruguay, go back to its independence in 1818, and the decades of the nineteenth and early twentieth centuries that followed.[2] Like Uruguay, Chile was a colonial backwater far from the centers of Spanish colonial power and exploitation in and around the Caribbean and the Viceroyalty of Peru.

Other Spanish colonies exploited gold and silver, but Chile and Uruguay had none. (Only later in the nineteenth-century, after wars with Bolivia and Peru, did Chile gain easily gathered resource wealth from guano and nitrites.) As a result, "scarcity and sobriety became the norm among government officials under colonial rule and ... established a precedent that survived after independence was achieved."[3]

The local ruling class in Chile before and after independence was European, and considerably influenced by the ideas of the Enlightenment (as in Scandinavia) and by Anglo-Saxon and North American liberal values. Its ideas of constitutionalism were derived less from currents of thought in Catholic-influenced southern Europe than they were from northern Europe and North America, their trading partners. Unlike the landowning elites in Argentina and Brazil, the patricians who helped to rule Chile in the nineteenth century lived in towns and cities more than on great estates. They also focused less on personal enrichment, and considered themselves stakeholders rather than all-powerful patrons and caudillos. These values helped to lean Chile and Uruguay toward attitudes approximating ethical universalism.

Leadership was decisive, too. Diego Portales was a George Washingtonian–type figure influential in Chilean politics in the decades after independence; he is credited with authoring the constitution of 1833. That constitution sought to establish strong institutions within a strongly centralized state, but—because Portales distrusted politicians and political maneuvering—it also was written to discourage the concentration of power in the hands of single individuals or small groups of cronies. That is the second reason why Chile entered the twentieth century without a tradition of "big man" rule. A 1925 constitution, after a period of instability, shifted power from the legislature to the executive, and thus further weakened the political dominance of Chile's landed oligarchy without contributing to an upsurge in corruption because rule-of-law institutions were also strengthened. The new constitution, signally, mandated life tenure until age seventy-five for judges (appointed by the president), and therefore put formidable foundations under the country's already-robust rule-of-law tradition. Of equal significance in this period, Chile established the Contraloría General de la República—an office of comptroller general or auditor general. (Its head was also appointed until age seventy-five by the president.) This powerful body was a bulwark against corruption, and its leaders were able by force of personality, and later because of Chile's competitive party system, to maintain an institutional independence even under military rule after 1973 until 1978, and then again after the restoration of democracy in 1990. Much more recently, Chile abolished its old system of investigating and prosecuting suspected criminals only under the order of judges. In 2005, Chile established a Fiscalía Nacional, a national prosecutor's office, to take charge of these functions and to help to decrease corruption. Ensuring fair competition and ending the kinds of oligopolistic practices that can lead to corporate corruption are now further assisted by these two additional twenty-first-century antitrust bodies.

Thanks to early and more recently revived leadership initiatives, Chile and Uruguay thus possess institutional safeguards against personal rule and kleptocratic aggrandizement. Their democratic political cultures are long established and domestically well regarded. Together, the collective behavioral expectations developed in the nineteenth century and the institutional barriers to chicanery—despite slippage from time to time—give both Chile and Uruguay an intolerance of grand and, certainly, petty corruption that is as Nordic in its focus as currently exhibited anywhere in South America. Nevertheless, this does not mean that during the twentieth century or now that either country was or is pristine in its political or corporate life.

Political vote buying was the norm in Chile, certainly during the 1930s and 1940s, and well into the 1950s. Patronage was rife, as it seems to have been in Uruguay during much of the same era. But Eduardo Frei Montalva and Salvador Allende, the presidents of the immediate period before Augusto Pinochet's coup, each strove with growing success to limit the roles of privilege and of purchased influence in politics. They could lead credibly because they were honest politicians of comparatively unblemished integrity. At the end of the twentieth century, their leadership and their efforts, and Chile's long-established institutional underpinnings of good governance, gave that nation an expectation of widespread accountability in the public sector, buttressed by a formidable rule-of-law culture tempered by acceptance of levels of corruption just below the threshold of public outrage.

Postrevolutionary Costa Rica

Just as Uruguay and Chile are significant outliers in South America, Costa Rica is strikingly dissimilar from its Central American neighbors in many important ways, not least in terms of its status as a comparatively noncorrupt country in Latin America and globally. Unlike Uruguay and Chile, however, Costa Rica's government was thoroughly corrupt in the nineteenth century. Holding public office was openly used for personal gain on a large scale. Prominent families competed for political positions in order to enrich themselves along with their cronies and clients. Two authorities call corruption in Costa Rica before the twentieth century, and even well into that century, "systematic and widespread."[4]

Nevertheless, Costa Rican exceptionalism then and now helped to propel the nascent state on a trajectory that was distinct from those of its neighbors. In 1869, Costa Rica introduced free, compulsory education. In 1889, it held a free and fair election, and witnessed the country's first peaceful transfer of power. Gradually, in the 1880s and 1890s, judges were given more and more autonomy, and congressional and executive interference became less burdensome.

Following the two-year dictatorship of Federico Tinoco Granados that ended in 1919, Costa Rican opinion shapers sought ways to curtail executive power, enhance judicial independence and overall accountability, and curb the corrupt excesses that had been central to the operations of the dictatorship. An Oficina de Control was established specifically to audit all governmental spending and especially contracts let by the executive. Those who overthrew the dictatorship also encouraged the emergence of a bold free press, specifically in order to enhance future accountability and transparency. Judges were given life tenure and guaranteed salaries, and the court system was gradually professionalized, especially after further reforms in 1935. Subsequently, the country's 1949 Constitution gave the judiciary the full independence that it enjoys today.

Even so, politicians still managed to enrich themselves by holding public office, and the purchasing of influence, permits, and major contracts (through kickbacks) remained features of Costa Rican political life. It took popular anger at the extent of political and corporate abuses to erupt (among other causes) into a major civil war in 1948. That war, and its democratic victors organized by José Figueres, led to Costa Rica's reconfiguration into the Central American exception that it now represents. The civil war and its aftermath in fact helped to change the country from a politically unstable democracy to a stable, consolidated democracy with competitive elections contested by ideas-based political parties. Costa Rica was transformed from an impoverished backwater to the most prosperous country in the region.

Drawing on the democratic ideas of Rodrigo Facio Brenes, a homegrown political conceptualizer consciously influenced by the Uruguayan political model and its successes, Figueres agreed to dissolve his victorious junta and to give the country's presidency to his major opponent. He and Facio persuaded the constitutional assembly to abolish the nation's standing army, to establish the weakest presidency in the Americas constitutionally, and to create a unique institution, the Tribunal Supremo de Elecciones (Supreme Elections Tribunal). Politically and financially autonomous, this last body controls all aspects of elections, including the training and staffing of poll workers, and also acts as the nation's registrar general for births, marriages, and the like.

The framers of the 1949 Constitution were intent on preventing coups, dictatorships, civil wars, and the kinds of large-scale fraud that had been common before the civil war. To those ends, the 1949 Constitution also inaugurated several new institutions to enhance accountability: the Contraloría General de la República (Comptroller General's Office), Procuraduría General de la República

(Attorney General's Office), and an audit agency, called the Bank Auditing Office, for the newly nationalized state agencies, which included the state banks and the country's electric utility. Subsequently, too, a law was passed in 1950 that mandated the declaration of assets by all public officials (later including judges). In 1973, in order further to insulate the executive from temptation, the prosecutorial office and the criminal police were placed under the authority of the Supreme Court. The Fiscalia was moved out of the executive branch and placed under the courts so that corruption (and other crimes) could be pursued more completely.

Of even greater importance was a 1989 reform that created a special (and again unique, except possibly for South Africa) Constitutional Chamber of the Supreme Court. This chamber has broad powers of judicial review. Its decisions are not subject to further adjudication, and it rather easily and widely grants standing to question the constitutionality of legislative and executive actions. It constitutes a useful watchdog against corrupt practices, and an institution before which civil society and individuals can present challenges to authority.

Despite these positive institutional developments, there were a plethora of corruption scandals during the 1990s and 2000s. Those incidents—largely but not exclusively involving the financing of elections, money laundering through national banks, peculation of official resources, and awarding of contracts for telephone, electricity, and aviation franchises and purchases—sometimes involved sitting and former presidents, legislators, and even the elections office itself. Some of the illicit monies came from Taiwan, and some of it came from drug smugglers. So despite the many institutional safeguards and the mostly valiant efforts of the press, corrupt behavior continued to some significant degree in modern Costa Rica through 2017. Although corruption was not the central issue of the 2018 presidential election, the overwhelming victory of center-left candidate Carlos Alvarado Quesada strengthened the hands of those in civil society who had been campaigning against homegrown corruption as well as the muted but nonetheless evident narco trafficking that spreads illicit money into all Central American politics. President Alvarado promised to battle any corrupt dealings that persisted despite these safeguards.

Together with a more vigorous free media and a more aroused civil society, scholars of Costa Rican corruption assert that a corner has been turned. Several new laws passed in the 2000s have helped and have been employed successfully to strengthen accountability. Judges in this century are better trained, and not drawn from political parties or ranks. There is an office of public ethics that acts to oversee the civil service and politicians, and petty corruption is absent in daily public and private interactions.

In 2018 and since, "Costa Ricans are ... highly sensitive to corruption, and corruption scandals are more frequently reported in the media. ... [C]ases are much more likely to be officially brought to public awareness on social media where they will be met with emphatic disapproval and even condemnation, which in time helps to make corruption less acceptable."[5]

Avoiding the Resource Curse

Neither Uruguay nor Chile has extensive oil deposits. But Chile is one of the world's greatest producers of copper. Uruguay relies on exports of beef and has some gold. Costa Rica exports bananas, pineapples, and coffee, and imports tourism. All three countries consequently have been spared being harmed by the resource curse, or "paradox of plenty," that too often leads countries rich in natural resources to experience stagnant economic growth and stunted democratic attainments due to the corruption of their leaders. In the Chilean case, allegations of corruption marred the final years of Michele Bachelet's presidency; candidates from her political party were accused of accepting illegal corporate contributions, and her son was accused of taking a large loan from a wealthy banker to purchase land that was expected to soar in value thanks to zoning decisions that could be influenced politically.

Nevertheless, Chile's vibrant press and reliable public institutions were resilient. No impunity resulted, and the country's reputation as a noncorrupt or minimally corrupt South American outlier survived the scandal. In 2020, despite the growing presence of narco traffickers, its institutions remain strong and uncaptured by criminal forces.

As a result of a series of political leadership actions in Uruguay, Chile, and Costa Rica during the twentieth century and more recently, the political cultures and peoples of all three Latin American countries are far less disposed to tolerating corrupt practices than their neighbors. This evolution away from an acceptance of corrupt dealings occurred because political leaders of different backgrounds and ideological persuasions charted noncorrupt courses in their respective nations, and nurtured an ethos in each country that was hostile to corrupt dealings.

CONFRONTING CORRUPTION
THROUGH LAWS AND COURTS

Standard doses of prosecutorial zeal, based on effective domestic laws, and presuming reasonably honest judges, were once thought sufficient to curtail corruption in most political jurisdictions. That was when researchers thought that the key problem was simply identifying the miscreants—the misbehaving agents—and hauling them off to jail, one by one. But now, decades later, we realize that those who oppose corruption within national societies cannot really presume that ferreting out corrupt principals and their agents can and will actually be accomplished within existing frameworks of justice, or be sufficient. We cannot be sure that special investigative commissions will do any better in revealing those who are corrupt or unmasking the many corrupt schemes that may bedevil the government of, say, a fragile state. In most of the largely corrupt regimes globally, it would be wrong to take investigative or prosecutorial skills for granted; it would be wrong to assume sufficient political will to pursue those who are questioned and even indicted on suspicion of corrupt dealings. Historically, and with few exceptions, it has never been, and is not now, a simple matter to discover corrupt behavior and then to bring the culprits to the bar of justice. Indeed, for society in general to array itself against corruption, it needs a variety of imaginative mechanisms as well as methods to unearth and then to deter corrupt acts. It requires good laws, good investigatory instruments and techniques, careful auditors, dedicated ombudspersons, a fully free and active media, appropriate operating judiciaries, and some new types of courts. Conscientious and principled leadership is essential.

Legal Frameworks

Nearly every nation-state outlaws corruption, in almost all of its guises. The best legal codes define corrupt acts and behaviors clearly, spelling out what is licit and what is illicit. The laws of some countries even specify, in some detail, monetary limits on gifts that may be given to and received by public servants, and under what conditions. Some national legal frameworks, however, are general, vague, ambiguous, or imperfectly drafted (with too many loopholes).

A few of the most anticorrupt states, after finding existing legislation too permissive, have written the toughest kinds of laws to ensnare corrupt offenders. The result, designed to ease the pursuit and prosecution of corrupt players, permits circumstantial matters to be introduced in court; suspects who are "living beyond their means" are capable of being prosecuted on those grounds alone. That usually means that the person or persons in question hold assets whose origins they cannot explain or justify, or own homes or motor vehicles (or yachts) more expensive than their public salaries could afford. Britain's National Crime Agency uses "Unexplained Wealth Orders" to compel big spenders and (presumably) major money launderers to show that their riches stem only from licit activities, not from corruption in their countries of origin. In several nation-states that have successfully reduced corruption, their prosecutors (to the dismay of civil libertarians) have been permitted to introduce hearsay evidence, and to infer guilt from suspicious actions and appearances. Hard proof has not necessarily been required.

Because in both the Singapore and Hong Kong city-states corruption had run rampant under British colonial rule—in both places corruption was a way of life, little interfered with by the colonial authorities—incoming administrations in the 1960s and 1970s, respectively, crafted strong anticorruption laws that are purposely more punitive and proscriptive than most. Singapore denies a number of protections that are fundamental to common law regimes in the British Commonwealth and the United States. For example, Singapore's 1960 Prevention of Corruption Act defined the offense in terms of "gratification." No one could borrow money or in any other way financially obligate herself to anyone with whom she had official business. Public servants also had to declare their assets annually, and could not be "entertained" in any manner by members of the public. In addition, Singaporean public servants could be prosecuted for corruption even if their offenses occurred abroad.

Punitive laws and aggressive enforcement significantly assisted Singapore's all-out attack on corruption. Suspects were not allowed to stay silent instead of incriminating themselves. Persons "reasonably suspected" of being crooked could be arrested without a warrant. Prosecutors could see the bank accounts of the accused as well as the accounts of all of their relatives. Givers and takers were equally culpable, and each merited stiff fines and imprisonment. They also had to repay the full amount of bribes received. Corrupt civil servants lost their jobs automatically.

Over the course of the years from 1960 to 1989, penalties were stiffened and new stipulations added. In 1966, for example, an accused could be found guilty of corruption merely for intending to commit the act, not for actually having done it. In 1989, the estates of culprits who had committed suicide to avoid public humiliation could be forfeited to the nation. So could the assets of anyone who fled Singapore to escape the police's reach. As recently as 2015, the Supreme Court of Singapore increased the prison sentence of a ship's inspector who had solicited bribes in order to forgo inspections even though the offender was a private person under contract, albeit performing quasi-governmental functions.

In Hong Kong, after it became clear that the nineteenth-century laws of the colony that prohibited various forms of corruption were inadequate, and that British officials had been conniving for decades with Chinese triads to enrich themselves and the gangs, a newly arrived British governor and his council passed a 1974 Prevention of Bribery Ordinance along with an updated Corrupt and Illegal Practices Ordinance. They also enacted an Independent Commission against Corruption (ICAC; see below). It consequently became illegal to obstruct justice, steal government goods, blackmail anyone, deceive others, make false accusations, or conspire with others to commit an illegal act such as bribery. Hong Kong criminalized "any act or omission in the discharge [of official duties] for the purposes of obtaining benefits for himself or herself or for a third party."[1] Kickbacks, unauthorized rebates, and any takings "of advantage" were prohibited. Civil servants would become suspect if they lived beyond "known means."

Like the Singaporean legislation, the new Hong Kong act permitted prosecutors to conduct searches, examine bank accounts and safe-deposit boxes, subpoena witnesses, audit private assets, seize passports, close borders to prevent escapes, and prevent monies being transferred outside the colony.

In South Korea after new legislation in 2015, it became illegal for public officials, teachers, and journalists to accept cash or gifts worth more than the equivalent of ninety dollars. Any transaction larger than the equivalent of ninety dollars was presumed to be a bribe. Gift giving and exchanging, two common South Korean practices, were banned between any public servants and their clients and customers. The spouses of public servants were intentionally presumed to be guilty along with the culprits, if they were civil servants.

Most of the laws against corruption in Africa are consciously copied from Hong Kong and Singapore. But as good and as thorough as the legislated prohibitions of corruption are, and accompanied as they are by schedules of robust fines and long years of imprisonment, in many cases political will has been weak or compromised, and corrupt offenders have not been pursued.

For example, in 2001, after lengthy investigations, Zambia's Anti-Corruption Commission decided that the minister of local government was taking bribes. A detailed indictment was presented to the director of public prosecutions, and then a long delay ensued. Eventually, the commission was informed that President Frederick Chiluba had ordered no prosecution and that the whole investigation should be quashed. (The minister in question, ironically, was Michael Sata, a longtime political operative who subsequently served as Zambia's president.) Sometimes, too, in addition to weak political will, the whole question of corruption is ignored by kleptocratic regimes, especially in criminalized states.

Even Botswana, long the least corrupt nation-state in Africa, had lapses in enforcement before scandals in the early 1990s led to the passage of the Corruption and Economic Crime Act of 1994, modeled on Hong Kong's legal framework, and an Ombudsman Act. The Corruption and Economic Crime Act outlawed the obtaining or receiving of gifts, benefits, rewards, loans, employment promises, discharges of loans, or "any other service" between citizens and officials. It further modified existing common law rules of evidence, and gave investigators the right to examine anyone who might be connected to or acting "conducive" to corruption. The existence of "unexplained or disproportionate resources" would prove grounds sufficient for arrest.

The Limits of Laws

Elsewhere in Africa, countries such as Tanzania, Zambia, and Ghana have stringent laws on their books. Tanzania's 1971 Prevention of Corruption Act, strengthened in 2002 and 2007, makes public sector corruption illegal and also uniquely prohibits corruption in the private sector. But few arrests or prosecutions have ever been attempted under the act. Judges have also been paid to ignore most infractions of the law. An Anti-Money Laundering Act (of 2006 and 2012) is intended to curb capital flight. The 2004 Public Procurement Act forbids illegal methods of influencing tender bids, but the Public Procurement Regulatory Authority has largely failed to stop fraudulent practices. The Election Expenses Act of 2010 bans the naked buying of votes (and more). A Public Leadership Code of Ethics orders public officials to file annual accounts of assets, but government officials falsify their declarations or routinely simply refuse to make disclosures. Tanzanian anticorruption legislation, sensible and formidable as it is on paper, has been ignored, evaded, and abused—as the 2014–2015 attempt by cabinet ministers and legislators to steal more than $122 million from the nation's electricity utility demonstrates. When President John Magufuli took power in 2015, he promised to oversee the enforcement of the country's strict laws and end corruption. But his high-handed rule ended up mostly benefiting himself and his coterie, with just as much corruption persisting in Tanzania in 2020 as in earlier eras.

Zambia in 2010 upgraded its existing anticorruption legal arsenal, several provisions of which are similar to Tanzania's. It also legalized plea bargaining, and explicitly penalized false testimony, the alteration of documents, and the obstruction of justice. In Ghana, it is an offense for public servants to allow themselves to be influenced by gifts or "valuable considerations." Police officers are guilty of extortion under the Criminal Code Act of 2003 if they demand money or "valuable considerations," but many still do, on a daily basis.

One of the best-drafted anticorruption legal codes is South Africa's Prevention and Combating of Corrupt Activities Act. Legislators, judges, and bureaucrats may not accept "gratifications," and are not allowed to expedite or prevent the performance of an official act. Investigators are permitted, as in most other African and Asian nation-states, to arrest suspects without notice and seize their assets.

All of these and dozens more illustrations of legal drafting against corruption in vulnerable states show that corruption persists not because of insufficiently strict and careful rules but rather because in the latter examples, like Zambia's, political will has been lacking. Presidents, prime ministers, cabinet ministers, attorneys general, and even judges have found legal strictures against corrupt behavior easy to evade or ignore. Civil societies have failed to influence most rulers to obey domestic anticorruption laws. In South Africa, with its comparatively strong political institutions and long official antagonism to corruption, it took the combined actions of an aroused public, a revealing report from the official public protector (ombudsperson), careful and prolonged media sleuthing, a telling judgment of the Constitutional Court, and a decisive political shift within the ruling party to disrupt or at least slow down the capture of the state by corrupt politicians and their private sector enablers. The existing legal framework eventually helped, but public awareness and criticism of the then state president's questionable activities and the vast amounts of state money spent on his private home in rural KwaZulu-Natal, ultimately forced President Zuma to resign.

International Enforcement Measures

Corrupt politicians, officials, and businesspeople run afoul of the legal instruments of their own domestic jurisdictions, and are prosecuted (in some instances) in their national courts. But what of those foreigners who pay lavishly and illegally for mining concessions, drilling rights, or lucrative construction contracts? There is a helpful Bribe Payers Index, which names the twenty-eight most offensive wealthy countries that export corruption. Even so, who has the authority to arrest those foreigners who tempt local public servants? Who, in other words, can seek to sanction the tempters and thus prevent temptation? Without supply, demand shrinks.

Aware of these realities, in 2003 the United Nations finally voted in favor of a Convention against Corruption (UNCAC) designed to ban corrupt behavior globally, including corporate behavior. It required members (178 states have ratified it) to repress corruption within their borders and to return monies laundered ("stolen") back to the appropriate nations.

The Convention against Corruption is toothless, however, as is the global industrial powers' Organization for Economic Cooperation and Development's Convention on Combating Bribery of Foreign Officials (1997). "Bribery," it declared, is harmful to the international "battle against corruption." The convention asked nation-states to pass their own laws criminalizing the bribing of host country nationals so as to reduce the insidious nature of supply-side corruption, and to do so forcefully even when bribes are solicited. "Have you brought something for me?" is meant to be answered by corporations and individuals in countries that have signed the convention with a resounding and horrified "no." That rebuff is intended to accompany and encourage transparent accounting practices, the abolition of the crime of false documentation, a lessening of bank sector secrecy, and new attitudes about extradition.

In these conventions, however, there is nothing other than shame and risks to reputation to dissuade potential corporate offenders from adding illicit inducements to any deals concluded between multinational behemoths and home-based developing world leaders. Instead, the major deterrents to developed world graft being inflicted on developing world leaders and their countries are the several important prohibitions imposed on their own corporations by the globe's major economic powers.

The ultimate arbiter of all of these attempts to curtail overseas bribery is the US Foreign Corrupt Practices Act (FCPA) of 1977 (amended in 1988 and 1998). The act makes it illegal for any publicly traded concern (and its officers and employees) to pay foreign governmental officials to obtain or retain business. This prohibition has been interpreted broadly to apply to US persons and corporations, to nominally foreign firms that bank or issue securities in the United States, and to concerns that have employed the US banking system.

In the first era of the FCPA, enforcement was a limited, rather half-hearted effort. But since the early years of the Obama administration, the US Department of Justice, in cooperation with the Securities and Exchange Commission (SEC), has actively pursued violators, whether American or not, won many convictions, and—arguably—

reduced the incidence of graft overseas. In late 2019, investigations of 135 US and 12 foreign corporations were underway, showing the Trump administration's continuation of Obama era zeal. Disgorgements and penalties paid in recent years amounted to several billion dollars annually; a number of individuals have been convicted in US courts for infringements of the act. In late 2018, Petrobras, at the center of the Lava Jato corruption trials, was penalized as much as $1.78 billion by the SEC.

In 2019, the SEC fined Walmart $283 million to settle allegations that the mammoth grocer had violated the FCPA by paying an intermediary in Brazil to obtain construction permits and for having weak anticorruption internal controls in China, India, and Mexico. In India, apparently, "concerns about bribery were met with a 'wink and a nod'" by Walmart's local partner.[2] In Mexico, the company gave computers and motor vehicles to communities where Walmart wanted to implant its stores. Through middlemen, Walmart made "dubious" payments to governments in a legion of countries outside of the US.

The Fortune 500 United Technologies Corporation, in a more typical case, agreed to pay the SEC $13.9 million to settle FCPA offenses related to its Otis Elevator and Pratt & Whitney aircraft engine businesses in China, Azerbaijan, and six other countries. In China, to gain aircraft contracts, Pratt & Whitney paid $55 million to one go-between, gave $2 million to another agent for "office renovations," and sponsored a golf tournament with substantial gifts to participants. In Russia, Otis permitted municipal officials to falsify documents. In Azerbaijan, a senior local official involved in approving elevator procurements purchased for himself, as an investment, four apartments in Istanbul worth almost $2 million.

Earlier, in 2017, the Swedish telecommunications company Telia paid the SEC $965 million to settle charges concerning its bribery of Uzbek officials. The US Department of Justice also froze $1 billion in corrupt assets obtained by Gulnara Karimova, daughter of Uzbekistan's then dictator and the key orchestrator of the Telia scheme.

The United States also employs the Global Magnitsky Act, an antikleptocracy effort enacted in 2016, to pursue and punish those who engage in grand corruption and its accompaniment, human rights violations. (Britain, Canada, Estonia, Latvia, and Lithuania have passed similar laws.) Under Global Magnitsky, the US government imposes visa bans and freezes assets in the United States to punish human rights abusers as well as corrupt foreign officials and their associates. This act applies specifically to anyone engaged in "significant corruption, including the expropriation of private and public assets for private gain, corruption related to government contracts or the extraction of natural resources, bribery," and the laundering of monies.[3]

The British Bribery Act of 2010, along with similar relatively recent legal bans by Australia, Austria, Canada, Finland, France, Germany, Israel, Italy, the Netherlands, Portugal, and South Korea, mirrors the enforcement and prevention possibilities of the FCPA. It is joined by Britain's 2016 Criminal Finances Bill, which compels suspected criminals and money launderers to explain the sources of their wealth, and, if questionable, have their property seized. Canada's Corruption of Foreign Public Officials Act of 1998 applies only (unlike the broader FCPA) to Canadians.

The passage of these various restrictions on the corruption of public servants by (mostly) multinational corporations from the developed world is a distinctly twenty-first-century innovation. But, as late as 2020, only in a few of the listed countries was the investigation and prosecution of offenders as vigorous as it has been under the FCPA. Canada, for example, has prosecuted only a handful of relatively blatant suspects, with but four convictions between 1998 and late 2019. French and Dutch governmental activities in this area have also been notably restrained, but in 2019 the United Kingdom's Financial Conduct Authority imposed the equivalent of more than $300 million worth of fines on individuals and firms, trebling its previous year's actions.

Because the FCPA deals with the supply side of corruption, several US congresspersons in mid-2019 tabled a new bipartisan bill that, if passed, would also penalize those who solicit bribes and other illicit payments from US corporations. The proposed Foreign Extortion Prevention Act would allow the US Department of Justice to indict overseas officials who demand bribes. It is akin to existing legislation already enacted in France, the Netherlands, Switzerland, and the United Kingdom.

The World Bank employs a simpler method than prosecution to deter multinational corporations from bribing public servants in the developing world. When the World Bank's Integrity Vice-Presidency has sufficient evidence of corporate malfeasance, it simply bars the offenders from bidding on World Bank–financed contracts for three to ten years. In recent times as many as 650 entities, mostly construction concerns, were thus blacklisted—in one Canadian case, for 115 offenses. It had bribed to win tenders for a bridge over the Ganges River, in Bangladesh, and for a rural electrification scheme in Cambodia. The World Bank forbade SNC-Lavalin to apply for projects for ten years.

Similarly, in late 2019 the Inter-American Development Bank barred Odebrecht and nineteen of its subsidiaries from bidding on that bank's projects for six years. Odebrecht admitted paying $118 million in bribes from 2007 to 2015 to secure two major bank-financed contracts for a major road construction opportunity in Brazil and a key hydroelectrical facility in Venezuela. It had earlier been penalized $2.6 billion by US authorities, Brazil, and Switzerland for its involvement in the Petrobras and other scandals. In late 2019, too, Odebrecht filed for bankruptcy with $25 billion in debts.

In Europe, the European Investment Bank has a robust Fraud Investigations Division that examined 149 allegations of corruption by its (mostly) large corporate borrowers in 2017 and 184 in 2018. It uses a Fraud Risk Scoring Model to select projects subject to proactive integrity reviews—to oversee activities that might be prone to being corrupted.

An International Anticorruption Court

Judges in all jurisdictions, even the least corrupt, are sometimes swayed by political reality. Whether they adhere in their minds and hearts to the impartial principles and procedures of the common or Napoleonic civil laws, they are sometimes moved to favor the wishes of those who pay their salaries or control their preferment and promotions. Where the national executive or legislature hold the budgetary reins, where the executive intervenes forcibly concerning the outcomes of individual cases, and where autocrats decry the rule of law, it is exceedingly difficult even for the bravest of judges to exercise impartiality and obey the dictates of their judicial consciences. For example, under President Mugabe in Zimbabwe in 1999, a high court judge ordered the minister of defense to release two journalists held by the army. Mugabe quickly overruled the judge and notoriously opined that "the law is what I say it is."[4]

When and where regimes destroy judicial independence, forfeit obedience to an evenhanded rule of law, impede peaceful dispute resolution, undermine the credibility of contracts, take property willy-nilly, and discard due process—all on account of entrenched corruption—then foreign investors and potential aid donors become wary, economic growth prospects suffer, and homegrown remedies are absent or unusually difficult to implement. Furthermore, absent an affirmative judicial climate, curtailing corruption—even minimally—becomes highly compromised.

If kleptocracy prevails and the courts are thus compromised—for whatever set of reasons, and no matter to what degree—prosecuting authorities are in cahoots with the dominant domestic actors, and there are no internal remedies available in any pragmatic sense, then some manner of outside intervention or mediation may be required. That external oversight could come most directly in the form of a new institution such as the proposed International Anti-Corruption Court (IACC).

Any IACC-type institution would sensibly focus its energies on the curtailing of grand corruption, leaving petty corruption to be limited by domestic police systems and legal enforcement efforts. But grand corruption of the venal kind most responsible for contract fraud, money laundering, large-scale theft from the public purse, and deleterious educational, public health, and infrastructural disasters can only be pursued and prevented by investigators and prosecutors who are loyal to an impartial institution independent of any domestic, thoroughly implicated, ruling clique. That could be an IACC authorized and legitimized by the UN General Assembly, or by a special convention or treaty analogous to the Rome Statute that established the International Criminal Court (ICC).

The IACC, wherever it might be based, would be mandated to investigate and prosecute heads of state along with other suspected senior-level kleptocrats and rent-accumulating rulers who preside over compulsively corrupt regimes and thus are beyond the reach of any (beholden) domestic judicial systems. The convention or other mechanism that established and empowered such a court would stipulate whether or not an IACC would have the ability to refer kleptocrats to itself when it determined that local procedures were inadequate and whole populations were suffering. The convention might also declare that only the UN Security Council or the UN High Commissioner for Human Rights could authorize interventions absent local requests. The empowering formula might restrict the IACC's jurisdiction only to those instances where the offending country and its odious ruler voluntarily requested the oversight and involvement of the IACC. Complementarity, which is what this arrangement is called in international law, may prove as fundamental to the operations of an IACC as it has, unfortunately, to the running of the ICC. (Under this formula, the nations that never ratified the Rome Statute that established the ICC are free from its attention unless and until the ICC is authorized by the UN Security Council to proceed. In the case of former President Omar al-Bashir in the Sudan, a nonsignatory, the ICC could not investigate his alleged crimes against humanity until the Security Council gave its OK. In 2018, the ICC attempted to work around this kind of constraint when it began to investigate the actions of Myanmar, another nonsignatory, in the pursuit of alleged genocidal attacks on its Rohingya population. The ICC took the position that because Bangladesh was a signatory, and because nearly all Rohingya had been compelled to flee from Myanmar to Bangladesh, it could investigate.)

Alternatively, an authorizing method more effective than that created for the ICC might be found to make the operations of an IACC comprehensive and inclusive. Because frail and failing nation-states across the globe often find it difficult forensically to investigate and thoroughly follow the tortuous and devious trails that would-be kleptocrats and other venal politicians make across their own national as well as international terrains, the IACC would preferably be staffed by the kinds of trained personnel and experts that most developing countries lack. That level of capability would hence be able to assist authoritative bodies in corrupt polities that sought help in following their own local cases. Or they could employ it to recommend cases for further investigation and possible prosecution. Established IACC staff would also be able to pursue flows of ill-gotten funds across national borders and "follow the money" more generally. Even if the IACC's annual load of cases was small, because of jurisdictional issues, its ability to name and shame could be powerful, and greatly contribute to the moral strength of world order.

The IACC's judges could ideally come from any approving and ratifying country. Like the judges of the World Court, they would be chosen for their legal experience and proven quality, and because they were deemed capable of providing wise oversight to the judges of the many domestic jurisdictions wholly or partially influenced by corrupt heads of state, or those court systems located within countries controlled by criminal, criminalized, or kleptocratic regimes.

If the IACC had existed in important cases, for example, it would have been able to weaken the hegemonic influence of local prosecutorial and judicial systems. An IACC investigation, authorized by the Security Council, would have had the authority to bring a despotic regime's various kleptocrats (including someone like President

Mugabe in Zimbabwe) before the court for trial. In the absence of an IACC, such corrupt officials are largely able to avoid punishment entirely.

Exactly how the issues that would have bedeviled any attempt to follow the money in the Zimbabwe case, or in the similar cases of the Democratic Republic of Congo, Myanmar, Nigeria, or even South Africa, are resolved—when and if the IACC is constituted—will determine its success and its utility in the corrupt remaining decades of the twenty-first century. There is little doubt, however, that some institution like the IACC is much needed, and that its existence and judicial ability to help corral and punish corrupt political leaders everywhere, plus the major searchlight on such activity that the IACC would represent, could help importantly to chill corrupt behavior by heads of state and their ilk everywhere. Opponents of the court are mostly those political leaders who might be investigated by such a court. Others worry that it might suffer from the same flaws as have beset the ICC. But the ICC's missteps as well as its prosecutorial errors and weaknesses could be avoided.

STRENGTHENING ACCOUNTABILITY AND TRANSPARENCY

In addition to bringing allegedly corrupt politicians and officials before tribunals so that they may be judged and, if merited, fined and sent to prison, there are a number of other constituted instruments that today's least corrupt nation-states have used and continue to use in their energetic attempts to reduce the stain of sleaze within their borders. Critically, they—and nation-states that want to follow their anticorrupt lead—most of all need to develop or invent methodologies that identify the grand corrupters from mere opportunists, reliably uncover the main perpetrators of domestic influence peddling for cash, and deter citizens and foreigners who believe themselves above the law—who believe that they can purchase the commercial or other favors that they need to prosper.

Catching the crooks is much harder than it seems. Few keep books. Few allow records to be kept. Handshakes and winks substitute for signatures. Bundles of cash may be spirited off—hence the need in most political jurisdictions to establish one or more ways of doubling down on accountability and transparency.

Investigative Commissions

A special-purpose body to investigate and bring to justice persons suspected of engaging in corrupt dealings is an obvious innovation, especially since the police and similar units normally charged with pursuing and preventing malefactors are often themselves enablers and participants in such nefarious activities. Singapore, where the police bosses were in cahoots with Chinese gangs to fleece businesspeople and citizens through all manner of corrupt acts, and where police detectives routinely doubled as thieves and opium smugglers and ran protection rackets, was among the first of the emerging new independencies to create a Corrupt Practices Investigation Bureau independent of the police. But it was largely ineffective in reducing rampant corruption in the city-state until Lee became Singapore's first independent leader in 1959. He introduced strong laws (see chapter 5) and remade the bureau into a fully motivated enforcement agency.

The bureau, as Hong Kong's later commission, received tips and complaints from whistle-blowers inside the administration as well as from the public. It followed additional leads to locate persons suspected of abusing their positions as public servants for private gain. When the bureau had developed sufficient evidence on which to recommend prosecution, it gave its dossiers to the attorney general's office for action.

On their own, the full-time British and local Malay and Chinese civilian investigators of Singapore's bureau might, over time, have uncovered enough evidence of malfeasance in the public service, port, banks, and industry to have reduced the city-state's wild levels of corruption. But behind and in front of them was Lee, the first prime minister of Singapore. He made sure that the bureau had sufficient funds and motivated personnel. He also kept the issue before the public in telling and important ways. As will be discussed below, Lee's demonstrations of political will complemented and helped to ensure the success of the bureau in its initial years—even before citizens of the city-state fully believed in its ability to carry out its mission.

By 2003, the bureau was completing 99 percent of its investigations within ninety days and winning convictions 85 percent of the time, admittedly with the cooperation of a compliant court system. This meant that by the end of the twentieth century, forty years after its inception, the bureau's work had become routine. The city-state, thanks to the bureau's early efforts, Lee's massive support and leadership, his autocratic and conformity-inducing rule, and effective legal formulas, had replaced an earlier culture of corruption with a political culture of integrity. Ethical universalism prevailed.

In the 1970s and 1980s, Hong Kong's ICAC elaborated on and extended some of the work of Singapore's bureau. Indeed, the ICAC became the model investigatory implementer, and the exemplar copied at least on paper by innumerable administrations in Asia and Africa. Its activities within Hong Kong showed what a well-led and well-conceived quasi-governmental body could do to limit corruption if conditions were otherwise ripe and political will were supportive of the commission's mandate.

Like Singapore, Hong Kong under British rule had been rife with corruption. Officials at all levels received tribute as a matter of course; otherwise the bureaucrats—the mandarinate—never budged. Illicit gambling flourished. There were brothels, dubious pawnshops, and questionable activities of every imagination catering to the desires of Hong Kong Chinese and non-Chinese alike. Criminal gangs profited from extortion. Bribery was a daily pursuit, often involving the colony's British, Indian, and local police heads. Even sanitary inspectors were bribed to look away. No construction project—no road, bridge, or harbor improvement—could escape its "extra" fees. None was immune from payoffs and kickbacks.

Hong Kong showed
what a well-led and
well-conceived quasi-
governmental body
could do to limit
corruption if conditions
were otherwise ripe
and political will were
supportive of the
commission's mandate.

By 1973, long after independent Singapore had begun to root out corruption, the British Hong Kong colony still suffered severely from the criminalization of its public service and its awkward position on the edge of a China seized by the Cultural Revolution. "Corruption was deeply rooted, widespread, generally tolerated [and] every part of the public service was infected."[1] It took an exposé in a prominent local financial journal and the flight from the colony of Peter Fitzroy Godber, a British police senior superintendent heavily implicated in local graft, to turn the administration from complacency and complicity to a determination to attack corruption.

Sir Murray MacLehose, the British governor, was committed less on moral than on practical grounds to clean up the mess that his predecessors had left for him and to eliminate as much corruption as possible. MacLehose's determination to act boldly and authoritatively may have been influenced by Hong Kong's situation as a supposed democratic, capitalistic outpost (with an ideology and reputation to uphold) adjacent to a Communist autocracy. He may have appreciated what Singapore, a similarly sized polity with British roots, had accomplished in a mere decade. He was keen, he said at the time, to establish the credibility of the colony's government and to build trust among its people.

The governor understood that public confidence in his administration was absent because of the long history of corruption. He also appreciated that the police could no longer be allowed to investigate themselves. So, building on Singapore's example, he created a wholly independent entity, the ICAC. The commission was empowered to uncover and pursue persons alleged to be corrupt, to prevent corruption by counseling against personal or ministerial behavior that could approximate corruption, and to educate the public against following or tolerating corrupt pursuits.

The ICAC reported only to the governor, immediately establishing its independence and ensuring its budgetary support. It also decided not to initiate investigations on its own; rather, it insisted on investigating all complaints of whatever kind delivered to it by the public, the better to demonstrate its impartiality. Citizen review panels provided oversight and guidance.

The commission could detain and interrogate suspects, confiscate their passports, view their bank statements, inquire about any unexplained displays of wealth, issue subpoenas, and arrest suspects. But it had to transfer cases to the public prosecutor for final presentation to a court.

By 1977, the ICAC operated in full force. It indicted a drug gang that had been paying the police $10,000 a day for protection; it further soon examined twenty-three large Chinese syndicates, eighteen of which were police run. Later, it charged hundreds of police officers with corruption, leading to arrests and trials. By 1980, the ICAC had succeeded enduringly to limit the pursuit of illicit gain by the police. It was also reducing the influence and standing of the main triads, and was beginning to move against culprits in the commercial sector. Ordinary citizens were seeing relief from the tolls that they had long been forced to pay to corrupt officials. In its first ten years, the ICAC developed about three thousand cases for prosecutorial action; 70 percent of those persons were convicted.

But as salutary as was the reestablishment of control over corruption and the rounding up of the usual miscreants, the ICAC's other major tasks—prevention and education—were also starting to produce outstanding results. Over the course of a number of years, the ICAC visited all government ministries and other public institutions. It explained how corruption had become outmoded as well as illegal, and what the members of a particular administrative entity could and should do to extirpate corrupt practices. It also examined the workings of every corner of the Hong Kong bureaucracy, and recommended ways of improving its dealings with the public and enhancing its patterns of operation so as to remove opportunities for corrupt behavior.

The ICAC's educational wing did the same throughout the colony's schools, helping teachers to introduce anti-corruption modules and, in general, finding a number of ways of using schooling to acculturate the next generation to be much less tolerant toward corruption than earlier ones. It also talked to businesses, determined to convert them into backers of the new dispensation rather than enablers. "Underhand dealings," it explained, "with an employee of a private sector business are not ... less reprehensible than underhand dealings with a civil servant."[2] As soon as 1986, according to a survey done for the ICAC, 72 percent of Hong Kong's citizens knew that they need no longer pay public servants extra just to perform their regular duties.

By the late 1980s, the ICAC's existence and methods had reformed the running of the Hong Kong Stock Exchange, reduced the falsification of accounts by major banks, curtailed arms and narcotics trafficking, and improved the way that lawyers went about their daily business. (Touting [aggressive soliciting] and illegal commissions had previously flourished; bribing judges had been common.) More than twelve hundred local firms had adopted strict corporate codes of conduct. The ICAC ended race fixing at the Royal Hong Kong Jockey Club as well. By 1997, when Hong Kong became a special administrative region of China, the city-state was experiencing vastly less corruption than it had in 1973. The triads were gone, the corrupt police force had been reformed, corporate life was mostly free of large-scale taint, and a spirit of ethical universalism prevailed. As a financial center, Hong

Kong had also benefited from its noncorrupt status. Clean business had proved positive for profits.

That same spirit continued until recently, even under increasingly tight Chinese control; Hong Kong remained an oasis in Asia of probity until 2019, when young Hong Kongers took to the streets in protest against Beijing's increasing dominance. Until then it had been a sentinel of anticorruption and an example to its neighbors. The ICAC also continued until 2019 to function much as it had long done: preventing, educating, and successfully prosecuting private as well as public persons—even those who (in one case) once helped to run the colony. Hong Kong's investigating commission showed how a model independent quasi-government entity could make a major difference, long term, in the interminable global struggle against the scourge of corruption.

The commission method, frequently modeled directly on Hong Kong's example of its organizing mandate and procedures, spread widely, especially in the 1990s and since. Indonesia and Croatia have powerful commissions capable of checking, if not eliminating, corrupt behavior in their countries. At one point earlier in this century, the leaders of Indonesia's Komisi Pemberantasan Korupsi (Corruption Eradication Commission, or KPK) could claim because of its efforts that Indonesia was freer than it had been historically of graft, peculation, and other corrupt ills. Senior politicians were jailed in the post-Suharto period; the KPK could assert credibly that its actions had disrupted the easy manner by which a generation of politicians and officials had abused their positions for private gain. But, with weak national political leaders and intense competition for patronage, by 2015 there was reduced national reliance on the KPK, and vigorous contests for political primacy between the KPK and a host of powerful military and political opponents. Corruption resurged despite the KPK.

Forty of forty-nine countries in sub-Saharan Africa alone adopted the Hong Kong model. But they did so often with fewer resources and, except for the commissions in Botswana and Mauritius, without the support of Lee-type leaders capable of ensuring the various commissions' integrity. Supported mostly by external donors, the African adoption of the Hong Kong model rarely translated well. For without supportive political will at the top of the various domestic political pyramids, the investigative endeavors of most of the commissions in Africa were curbed by their political bosses. The commissions were mandated to catch those who were corrupt; sometimes they did, but the attorneys general and other prosecuting authorities to which they had to surrender their cases for trial often decided to drop those cases without prosecution. Or they bungled the evidence as it had been presented, on orders from the various statehouses. In other words, the commissioners in Africa tried to do their job but, without much backing from dominant parties or long-lived rulers, their efforts were hindered at every turn. Political survival for the attorneys general trumped the pursuit of justice.

For the most part, too, the important tasks of prevention and education were largely ignored by the numerous commissions in Africa. Mauritius's own twenty-first-century direct copy of the Hong Kong model even carried the same name as its Hong Kong counterpart. Its commission could investigate various kinds of corruption, even covertly, and was also expected to educate the general public against corruption. But as formidable as the Mauritian commission tried to be, it was accountable to a committee of Parliament and could hardly function independently. Nor could otherwise-comprehensive commissions in Zambia and Malawi that were even run, for a time, by British expatriates reporting directly to the national presidents; they could never persuade their respective attorneys general or prosecuting authorities to pursue the tough cases—the corrupt dealings of members of the ruling party or cronies of the head of state.

Many promising investigations were quashed by respective state presidents. In one prominent Nigerian case, President Umaru Musa Yar'Adua sacked the head of the Economic and Financial Crimes Commission just before he was about to propose indictments of key politicians from the then ruling coalition. Already, Nuhu Ribadu, the commission's chief, had angered corrupt elites close to the president by successfully convicting 250 offenders and recovering $250 million in illicit gains. He even had the temerity to prosecute governors of influential states, the daughter of the president, a key senator, and an inspector general of the federal police. One governor of an oil-rich state forfeited $7.9 million. But, after being removed from office by Yar'Adua, this courageous commission head's replacement was forbidden to develop cases without the permission of the new minister of justice. In Nigeria, and elsewhere in Africa except for Botswana and Mauritius, these kinds of impediments meant that nearly all of the valiant commission attempts in Africa ended up being mostly futile exercises.

Employing a specialized investigative agency separate from the police to focus on corruption as a societal ill makes good sense. Backed by the will and actions of national political leaders, it presents a powerfully disruptive weapon to be employed against corruption in all of its many subversive postures. Yet, as dedicated and efficacious as the commission model has been in a handful of instances, the idea of impartially acting to bring highly placed corrupt politicians to justice proved too much to tolerate in many nation-states. At least as much as voters welcomed the assertive actions of commissions, so political elites hampered or dismantled effective commissions. Unlike the Hong Kong and Singaporean examples, many of the investigatory commissions elsewhere in the world functioned more cosmetically than not. Nevertheless, the investigatory commission model remains a strong potential tool, if deployed without interference, in the struggle to contain corruption.

Specialized International Commissions

Whereas dedicated domestic investigatory commissions have only in a relatively few instances succeeded irrefutably in unmasking corruption in their city-states (Singapore and Hong Kong) as well as in nation-states such as Botswana, Indonesia, and Mauritius, and, for briefer periods, Nigeria and Ghana, they still remain an unquestioned method of pursuing corrupt malefactors and, if following Hong Kong's example, educating governmental ministries and whole populations about the evils of condoning corruption. The tool itself is excellently crafted. How it has been wielded (and blunted) in many countries, however, betrays opportunities forfeited and progress forestalled.

More powerful, and in many ways an instrument less likely to be abused or diverted from its key purpose, is an investigatory commission sponsored and funded by an international organization. That was the origin in 2007 of the specially established UN International Commission against Impunity in Guatemala (CICIG). Created at Guatemala's request after years of brutal civil war to help eliminate injustices of all kinds and to transform political institutions in the country so that criminals could be held to account, it was headed from the start by prosecutors and judges from elsewhere in Latin America (most recently from Colombia). A tightly negotiated partnership between the United Nations and the government of Guatemala, the CICIG's mandate was to strengthen and assist Guatemala's efforts to identify and dismantle illicit criminal groups and menacing criminalized gangs terrorizing citizens within the country. Corrupt public servants were but one target; the CICIG was tasked with trying to solve many of the complex enforcement problems with which Guatemala's ethnically and class-embattled society could no longer cope.

Vicious cycles of impunity were central to Guatemala's paralysis of justice. Impunity for high officials like presidents and cabinet ministers sanctioned a vast web of criminalized and narcotics-connected corruption that was endemic and very difficult to eradicate. Indeed, as so many internal critics and external observers have noted, by 2007 corruption had infiltrated all levels and sectors of government and administration; no governmental institution was free of corruption. Rules of law were honored only in the breach, and at the whim of corrupt supposed public servants whose actions and interactions with citizens were largely governed by rent-seeking criminal syndicates run by state presidents and their cronies.

The CICIG was conceived as an independent new institution responsible for both investigating and prosecuting all manner of serious crimes in Guatemala. Its independence was unique and salutary for a country where objectivity and impartiality had long been rare. It supported the Office of the Public Prosecutor, and worked closely with the leaders of the national police force and with magistrates and judges. At the beginning, the CICIG sought to strengthen Guatemala's own judicial apparatuses, and to work with and not ahead of those seeking to uphold the rule of law, to interfere with criminals and corrupt actors, and to reduce impunity. It led investigations of vigilantism and all manner of criminal and criminalized behavior. It helped local agencies dismantle criminal networks. It recommended critical upgrades to the state's management of its prosecutorial and judicial functions.

This last role led for a time to striking improvements in Guatemala's own willingness to take on corrupt state officials. Reformers, supported by the CICIG, ran the attorney general's office and made impressive strides against impunity. According to Claudia Escobar, a local judge who eventually had to flee the country because of her refusal to take bribes, "Without the presence of the CICIG, nobody could have imagined that the president, vice president, members of the military, high government officials, politicians, powerful business men, and even judges would go to trial on corruption-related charges."[3]

In 2015, after the CICIG reported that the state's customs agency had received millions of dollars in kickbacks in exchange for reducing import duties and had delivered much of that bribe money to President Otto Pérez Molina, a former head of military intelligence, thousands of protesting citizens took to the streets and eventually forced Pérez's ouster. Additionally, the CICIG found that Pérez had presided over a massive scheme to profit personally from kickbacks from at least 450 construction contracts. He was at the head of a kleptocratic conspiracy intent on monopolizing the national revenue stream.

The CICIG also revealed (or confirmed public knowledge) that drug traffickers were financing politicians and political campaigns. It indicated from its undercover work that Guatemala's national social security financing scheme was fraudulent, too, and found a trail of suspect payments to political figures. Furthermore, the CICIG disclosed that the officials in charge of the national health system had skimmed millions of dollars off a contract meant to pay for dialysis treatments for patients with serious kidney complaints. That kind of negligence in the health system had led to loss of life.

Pérez was forced out by protesting masses, but so was the vice president (also implicated in graft), the head of the central bank, the head of the social security establishment, and several cabinet ministers. What the clear-minded investigations of the CICIG's team had done was to detail a long dossier of peculation and chicanery and, consequently, to unite Guatemalan citizens against corrupt leaders. An ensuing election brought new, supposedly much cleaner persons into high public office. (President Jimmy Morales, elected overwhelming in 2016, nevertheless attempted in 2019 to undermine the CICIG by sacking its chief prosecutor. Later, he refused to renew the CICIG's mandate. The commission was investigating Morales and his family for graft.) The CICIG ceased to exist in late 2019, thus ending a successful, if impermanent anticorruption experiment.

The utility and power of an uncompromised body such as the CICIG, legitimated and backed from outside the fragile nation-state, provides important anticorruption lessons. In the many places around the globe that possess weak internal controls and subservient judiciaries, deterring large-scale corruption may best be accomplished by such special-purpose bodies with mandates that are not subject to local political considerations. In contrast to its much more compromised analogue in neighboring Honduras (the Organization of American States' Mission to Support the Fight against Corruption and Impunity), the Guatemalan commission, led in recent times by Iván Velásquez, boldly and fearlessly employed advanced forensic means to peer under many of the rocks of local fraud and embezzlement. Together with the actions of an aroused civil society, its findings led to effective prosecutions as well as to the ouster of heads of state and their associates.

A willingness to challenge domestic political syndicates was critical in the Guatemalan case, and may be so everywhere else that a United Nations, Organization of American States, or African Union investigating commission may be created. Externally run, staffed, and financed bodies along with all kinds of transnational and extrasovereign entities, if properly instituted and led, can have salutary effects on corruption in those polities where that scourge has infected all state organs or the state has been captured by criminal organizations. Even in those rare places where the legal mesh against corruption is already tight and reasonably well enforced, what is now needed everywhere are the kinds of zeal and care that have been demonstrated in recent years by courageous prosecutors and judges in Brazil and Colombia as well as by the leaders of such innovative instruments as the CICIG.

Auditors and Ombudspersons

Careful auditing, especially forensic auditing, can uncover likely instances of cheating by public officials for private gain. Just as the CICIG found "unexplained" expenditures and transfers in Guatemala's health and social security administrations, so a contracted firm's audit of Malawi's ministerial accounts found much about which to be suspicious. Even routine audits, if done with an expectation of finding questionable, potentially fraudulent items on the books or expenditures against nonexisting budget lines, can disclose false tendering, all manner of likely graft, and even what looks like systemic corruption.

In properly run polities, auditors scrutinize each and every governmental operation. Even in the developed world, they examine documentation for contracts to ensure that authorized procedures and regulations are followed, and that nothing suspicious has occurred. Independent auditors that have free rein to examine every transaction, expenditure, supposed disbursement, and wire transfer can at least make the cost of individual grand corruption greater and the risks of discovery more intense. Certifying integrity in government (and business) is a key task for auditors, especially for auditors who know that they work in shady surroundings where high-level corruption is likely.

During the Ebola epidemic in Sierra Leone in 2015, for example, the country's national auditor noted that millions of dollars that were needed to combat the epidemic had "gone missing," much of the missing monies involving ministries that had "lost track" of donor funds meant to combat Ebola, and as a result, had caused reductions in the quality of service delivery in the health sector. Patients died.

South Africa's auditors, to give another example, found in 2014 that its national government had "wasted" billions of rands (the local currency) and had made R26 billion (then US$2.6 million) in irregular expenditures, up by a third from the previous year. In a number of cities, key employees had fiddled contracts for infrastructural projects and supplies so as to benefit themselves. The auditor general condemned governmental business conducted "outside the controlled environment."[4]

In Kenya, the auditor general found in 2015 that only 26 percent of the government's financial statements were accurate; 16 percent were "misleading." The auditor general in a subsequent year noticed that the government could not account for a large proportion of its annual revenues, that the police were paying for empty offices, and that the army was buying military vehicles that were not operable. The sum of $2 billion had been transferred illegally by officers to an offshore bank.

Auditors everywhere are able to provide one more check on the rent-seeking impulses of public servants, just as they can within multinational enterprises. But in many of the more fragile countries worldwide, especially in countries prone to corrupt behavior by politicians, auditors general are limited by statute from disclosing their routine or other findings to the public. In most cases, the reports of auditors general are not produced in a timely fashion, and are delivered to the relevant parliament or legislative chamber. In controversial cases, therefore, inconvenient findings are often buried by the parliamentary committee responsible for oversight. Where they are (infrequently) opened to public and media inspection, they are often ignored or closed. In Brazil, however, and in some developed countries, official audits are quickly posted online for all to peruse.

Opponents of corruption within countries need the findings of their national audit offices to establish tight cases against the persons or institutions within their societies that are possibly more aggressive than their counterparts in soliciting cash or in-kind payments that could be considered corrupt. Auditors are able at least to pinpoint such infractions so that parliamentarians, if they are independent and bold, can pursue remedies. That is what Brazil's Corregedoria Geral da União (the federal inspector general's office) does routinely. For some time this office has audited a representative sample of municipalities annually, eventually visiting all of the nation's 5,570 cities and towns. Civil society can also use information obtained by audit to further investigations or support voices of concern.

In countries like Canada, South Africa, and Malawi, where at least a subset of parliamentarians understand the power of thorough audits, the annual reports of auditors general are passed to a special, usually opposition-led parliamentary accounts committee. This committee's helpful job is to examine the findings of an auditor general's report, and then to cross-examine the relevant ministries or officials when funds have been misspent or gone missing. Parliamentary accounts committees often tackle controversial issues and are capable in the best cases of examining possibly corrupt suspects, particularly if the report of the auditor general has highlighted discrepancies in, say, ministerial accounts. If the auditor general has indicated unusual disbursements, the public accounts committee can interrogate the potential culprits. It can also ask ministers why projects are late and service delivery prospects are questionable. If necessary, the committee's examinations, all done in public, can bring attention to misappropriations and other possible signs of corruption or calculated malfeasance.

The role in society and anticorruption advances of serious auditing protocols should never be underestimated. Nor should ancillary and complementary potentially anticorruption institutions such as that of offices of ombudpersons. In 2016 and 2017, the investigations and assertive reports of Thulisile Madonsela, South Africa's public protector, were salutary in converting citizen complaints into well-documented critiques that exposed President Zuma's spending excesses and likely corrupt behavior. Eventually, after a long battle between the governing African National Congress, Zuma, and Zuma's enablers, the public protector relentlessly outlined the extent of the president's probable self-dealing. Her ombudsperson efforts were capped in 2018 by Zuma's resignation as well as by some monetary restitution. A trial followed.

Few ombudspersons produce such impressive results on behalf of a nation. Yet, as an important institution in Europe, Africa, and Asia, ombudsperson offices entertain citizen complaints on a variety of subjects, most of which concern service delivery or the lack thereof. They constitute a crucial safety valve for the expression of grievances and the potential righting of wrongs. But as the public protector in South Africa demonstrated by thorough and careful investigation, and by force of personality, ombudsperson offices are able as well to become tribunes against corruption and other kinds of criminal paths pursued by politicians and other public servants.

The first ombudsperson was appointed by King Charles XII of Sweden in 1713 to watch over the performance of judges and bureaucrats, and to ensure that they remained loyal to the king. A century later, in 1809, Sweden's Riksdag established the Office of the Supreme Ombudsman to protect subjects of the king who might be unduly harassed and importuned by the chancellor of justice—the king's enforcer. But this early official—like so many of his contemporary successors—could expose harmful occurrences and suggest how infractions might be remedied, but he lacked the power to right wrongs directly. What the Swedish ombudsman could do, however,

Ombudsperson offices constitute a crucial safety valve for the expression of grievances and the potential righting of wrongs.

was to urge the Riksdag to enact legal changes that would remove whatever injustices he uncovered and, significantly, to identify likely instances of corruption. Sweden in the nineteenth century grew more and more interested in accountability for the state and its functionaries. The ombudsman expanded the duties of his office to meet this need.

Finland adopted the ombudsperson model in 1920, Denmark in 1954, and New Zealand in 1962. Those three countries and Sweden are usually deemed among the globe's least corrupt by the CPI (see chapter 2). Subsequently, the arbitrary and corrupt nature of many new national administrations led to the adoption of the ombudsperson model in the developing world. In 2019, Africa's fifty-four countries included forty-six with offices of ombudspersons.

Tanzania became the first African adopter, in 1965, with its Permanent Commission of Enquiry. Within a year, it was receiving three thousand complaints annually. Ghana and Mauritius soon followed with their own ombudsperson offices. Then, in 1973, Zambia and the Sudan created such positions, as did a number of Nigeria's now thirty-six states. Originally the president or governor in some of these jurisdictions appointed the ombudsperson, as King Charles XII had done. But later, and more customarily, poorly staffed African offices of ombudspersons were (under)funded by and reported to their respective parliaments. In practice that means that unlike the public protector in South Africa, most ombudspersons (mostly men) in Africa are largely constrained by their mandates as well as by the custom of their offices to hear complaints, investigate infractions of the law or procedure, and then (usually meekly) report their findings to parliament in writing. In too many cases, the issues on which they focus are petty (if individually important). Rarely do those ultimate reports lead to debates or discussions in parliament. Routinely, they are shelved, often without much public awareness or media dissemination. (Madsonela's successor turned out to be a loyal African National Congress functionary; her rulings were favorable to that political party, and heavily criticized by parliamentarians and judges.)

Only in Rwanda, where the ombudsperson's office functions as a de facto anticorruption commission, have African ombudspersons other than South Africa's undertaken direct investigations of corrupt behavior. But they could. It would be within their remit to examine possible peculation, failures of commission and omission, tender fraud, and particular abuses of official positions for private gain. If a country has an energetic and empowered ombudsperson, plus a free and inquisitive media, many likely forms of corruption can be exposed and transparency enhanced.

A Free Media

As Nelson Mandela said, "I cannot overemphasise the value we place on a free, independent and outspoken press. ... Such a free press will temper the appetite of any government to amass power at the expense of the citizen."[5] A free press and a free media are both essential if citizens hope to contain, or at least to combat, corruption. Absent the searching light of journalists and crusading editors, much that goes on behind closed government doors or in corporate corridors will remain dark, hidden from a public and, indeed, even inquiring minds within an administrative machine.

Kleptocrats, often autocrats, usually try to curb the activities of the media within and sometime outside their country. Too much scrutiny will reveal corruption or other illicit abuses of public office and, conceivably, arouse cynical and suspicious citizens. Or, in some situations, political leaders with lots to hide persuade wealthy "friends" to purchase and thus rein in overly inquisitive journalistic enterprises. That has happened in a number of Latin American nation-states as well as in Canada, South Africa, Sri Lanka, Myanmar, Pakistan, India, Russia, and the United States, among others.

Even easier, in some ways, governments that fear sunlight impose direct state control on broadcast media such as television and radio, or even own newspapers directly.

In Zimbabwe, the state directly publishes the largest two daily newspapers, owns the only television service, and controls the primary radio outlet. (Most Africans obtain their news from the radio.) It even, as in so many other countries, permits cell phones and SIM payment cards to be used only by registered persons. It has not managed directly to censor broadband or other internet services, as China, Cambodia, and other more technically proficient regimes have done. But Zimbabwe and other African autocracies periodically shut down all cell services for weeks, even months, at a time. More could come, along with other forms of interference.

The official Press Freedom Index prepared by Reporters without Borders rates 180 countries and puts Eritrea, North Korea, Turkmenistan, Syria, China, Vietnam, and the Sudan at the bottom of the list. Finland, the Netherlands, and Norway are at the top, with the United Kingdom in thirty-eighth place and the United States in the forty-first spot. (A recent study finds, moreover, that the pursuit of corruption in the United States is greatly hindered by its "news deserts": 20 percent of American newspapers have closed since 2004 and half of the nation's 3,143 counties are now covered by a single weekly. Almost two hundred counties have no press coverage at all. In such circumstances, accountability loses.)[6]

Media freedom is heavily compromised in such corrupt jurisdictions as Myanmar, Egypt, Turkey, and Venezuela, and throughout the rest of the Middle East and North Africa as well as sub-Saharan Africa. In Bulgaria, Malta, and Slovakia, journalists following the seamy trail of domestic corruption have been murdered, seemingly by hired killers. Saudi Arabia assassinated a critical journalist in its consulate in Istanbul. Criminal gangs in Mexico have dismembered reporters.

Botswana, Cape Verde, Ghana, Kenya, Malawi, Mauritius, Namibia, and South Africa are largely tolerant of media inquiries, but in authoritarian African countries such as Angola, Burundi, the Democratic Republic of Congo, the Sudans, and Togo, the media are heavily controlled and journalists find ferreting out information about questionable behavior perilous as well as difficult. In the likes of Brunei, Equatorial Guinea, and Eritrea there are no free media; free expression is heavily curtailed. In much of the developing world, in other words, performing a watchdog role and attempting to pinpoint losses of integrity (so that citizens can judge for themselves) is difficult and positively dangerous.

A Swazi editor was fired for exposing the prime minister's shady land deals. In South Sudan, a newspaper was shut after it suggested that the president's daughter was unpatriotic for marrying an Ethiopian. Turkey holds the record for jailing journalists. In Zimbabwe, two print writers were detained and tortured by the security forces when they asked questions about financial shenanigans.

Under a since-deposed Gambian dictator, death threats and middle-of-the-night arrests were visited on reporters who refused to sing the regime's praises. Zambia's president forced its main independent newspaper, which campaigned against graft, to shut down. All across the African continent as well as in Asia, and Latin America, there are innumerable examples of such intolerance of the fourth estate.

Where the media is interfered with, there is always much more corruption. The more draconian the restrictions imposed by anxious rulers, the more corrupt behavior there is to expose. Under those conditions, the work of newspapers and television and radio outlets is essential if civil society has any hope of holding corrupt political leaders and other public servants accountable. Transparency depends in part on publicizing the results of anticorruption activities as widely as possible. Shining a bright light is the first step in illuminating nefarious activities. The bright light also makes it difficult for public servants to steal, take kickbacks, favor friends, and so on.

One of the great triumphs of modern investigative journalism, comparable to the battle against graft and theft in Boss Tweed's New York at the turn of the twentieth century, occurred in Ghana in 2015. An enterprising reporter working for a local media company captured nearly five hundred hours of video that showed judges on the state's highest courts asking for bribes, extorting cash

Where the media is interfered with, there is always much more corruption. The more draconian the restrictions imposed by anxious rulers, the more corrupt behavior there is to expose.

from litigants in exchange for favorable verdicts, and negotiating the release of prisoners for stiff fees. Thirty-four judges and 150 other court personnel were consequently suspended and ultimately removed from their august positions. But their sackings did not necessarily mean that citizens in that country or in similar ones could count on the media elsewhere to help them keep track of and expose corrupt practices in all of their mendacious variety. Enterprising journalists are few, and the extent of corruption is vast.

One new nonprofit body adds considerably to the world order's ability to unearth often-hidden information about corruption and organized crime, and the devastating connections between them. The Organized Crime and Corruption Reporting Project (OCCRP) styles itself as an investigative reporting platform established by forty centers that rely on the sharp services of a number of journalists and regional news-gathering entities around the globe. From 2006 onward, the OCCRP has depended on a growing network of investigative reporters to expose corrupt and criminal activities across all continents.

According to its website, the OCCRP has "quietly become one of the world's largest investigative reporting organizations, generating more than 60 cross-border investigations per year. Our websites inform more than 6 million readers and viewers every month, and 200 million other readers and viewers have access through legacy media which publish our work. The ever-widening impact of OCCRP stories demonstrates that when enough people possess the right kind of information they can bring about the right kind of change." The OCCRP uses technology to enhance its investigative abilities and claims actively to be "reinventing" journalism.[7]

Additional simple expedients, such as what is called in the United States "freedom of information" laws and methods for employing court orders to extract government-held information, do not exist in an effective manner everywhere. Where they do, and where such orders are obeyed, actions can be initiated against corrupt entities and individuals. Usually, however, there are no easily available or even findable documents capable of suggesting avenues of inquiry to journalists. Incriminating evidence must therefore be found in a suspect's new wealth, extensive foreign trips, or association with suspicious criminalized elements. Sometimes, though, good sleuthing turns up actionable information about how public servants falsified accounts, presidents failed to pay taxes or evaded taxes by clever maneuvers (as even in the United States), did the shady bidding of superiors, or made decisions clearly against the public interest. Transparency in these kinds of instances depends on good gumshoe work by journalists and other investigators, and on mistakes made by corrupt perpetrators.

Occasionally in the developing world, citizen, corporate, or donor pressures encourage transparency. The media then may be allowed to examine governmental actions to see that such activity is in the public interest, as in Uganda. In democracies, budgetary and official expenditure information is readily available. But in kleptocracies, those kinds of data are too often hidden or falsified. Revealing suspicions or showing partisanship may even prove deadly.

Other Innovations

All innovations that improve transparency are valuable. That is why the removal of rules for the sake of rules, or rules for the sake of bureaucratic convenience, are best eliminated or minimized in the quest for implementations conducive to reductions in petty corruption. If public servants are themselves compelled to be transparent, if they as individuals are relieved of the ability to be arbitrary, and likewise to exercise willful discretion, their natural tendency to seek inducements to act favorably, or to act at all, will be reduced.

At another level, enabling domestic corporations to operate with fewer constraints and less red tape of all kinds will reduce the need for "backhanders" or other gifts to encourage favorable responses from authority figures who have the ability inherent in their public office to advance or hinder entrepreneurial success. To make graft at the customs post less likely, helpful reforms include flattening the number of duty classes and categories into which products and other goods may be placed. Further, tariffs of all kinds should be limited, and the differences between them shrunk; best of all would be the declaration of a single or a small handful of easily understood tariffs for all goods imported into a fragile nation-state. Flows of business would also be improved, together with fewer opportunities to corrupt or be corrupted.

Many countries, such as Georgia in 2011 and India in 2019, have successfully placed as many as possible of these kinds of transactions online to avoid the temptation of personal discretion leading to corrupt behavior. It is a fairly simple matter to renew driving licenses, request birth and marriage certificates, obtain building permits, and apply for environmental permissions over the internet or with a cell phone. Corruption crumbles before modern technology.

For grand corruption, where the manipulation of the process of bidding for and the awarding of construction contracts or mining concessions provides real riches for political leaders and their associates, an analogous process can provide necessary transparency and restore faith in the fairness of all such potentially lucrative transactions. The EITI has for several years attempted with growing

Enabling domestic corporations to operate with fewer constraints and less red tape of all kinds will reduce the need for "backhanders" or other gifts to encourage favorable responses from authority figures.

success to reduce corruption in this arena by opening up all payments to public inspection. Yet, ordinary construction contracts, and the kinds of clever false tendering that typified the Lava Jato episode, are not covered by the EITI. Some similar mechanism should be found to provide for public inspection of the contents of all agreements to finance infrastructural projects, no matter the nature of the contractor (whether a local or multinational corporation, or a foreign state such as China) or the level (municipal, provincial, and national) of the enterprise. In these ways, the procurement process, always susceptible to graft, may be monitored by civil society and, of course, by energetic representatives of a free media.

The Private Sector

Much of this book thus far has focused on public sector corruption; misusing elective or appointed *public* office for private gain is easily understood as an abuse of trust—a deep violation of public service obligations to citizens and the commonweal. But nonpublic behavior can also be corrupt and against definitions of the public interest. Corruption by private corporations and their principals falls into this expanded arena, but so do the corrupt dealings of quasi-public bodies such as the key athletic federations of FIFA and the International Olympic Committee as well as entities everywhere that run sporting venues, Hollywood extravaganzas, award ceremonies, and so on. Corporate executives and their underlings, and the organizers of almost every kind of public event, can be compromised. So can the leaders of large or small nonprofit and otherwise-benevolent NGOs such as the Red Cross. Corrupt practices in these realms can be as pernicious and destructive to citizen rights as purely state-centered corruption. Impartiality, so often honored only in the breach, is decisive in all of these spheres of life. Transparency International's expanded definition of corruption rightly refers to abuses of "entrusted power" rather than abuses by persons in public positions only.

Business and athletic federation bosses can bribe and be bribed (as the award of championship locations by FIFA demonstrates), indulge in kickbacks and other kinds of monetary rewards for favorites, and—in general and overall—behave in a variety of ways that unfairly or least nontransparently influence both public and private choice. Private wealth obviously has the power to distort priorities at every level and to substitute its own for majoritarian preferences. It does so by engaging in Petrobras-like schemes, buying the attention and decisions of policy makers, and indulging avaricious public servants. One thoughtful commentator also regards the largest contemporary global corporate concerns, particularly Google, Facebook, Amazon, and Apple, as behemoths that are inherently corrupt because of their immense wealth, and the baleful influence that each exerts on the actions and policies of nation-states. Being monopolistic, as these and other corporations are, means that they are corrupt, and that they distort public goods in order to benefit corporate expansion and, ultimately, private (not public) benefit. Such private bodies "bend public power to selfish ends." When corporations exceed a certain size and prosperity, they are "built to corrupt."[8]

In his own intuitive way, Governor MacLehose in Hong Kong understood many of these dangers. In addition to reducing the corrupt power of the triads and pre-1974 public servants, he and his associates authorized the ICAC to end abuses of the public trust by firms and industries within the then colony. The ICAC reformed the conduct of business by investigating and prosecuting high and low executives, but MacLehose also instructed the ICAC to educate businesspeople against indulging in corruption.

As an earlier chapter in this book indicates, multinational companies are among the globe's largest and most persistent bribe payers. The EITI was designed smartly to bring transparency to this sector, but it is not always effective; much escapes its mesh of restraint. Much even evades the fine-toothed detection of the FCPA and similar legal instruments in Europe.

Judge Moro advises companies to "do their homework," to denounce "requests or demands for bribes," and to implement the kinds of internal controls and account-ability screens that make such fraud and graft more difficult.[9] A former US corporate lawyer, however, says that even the best internal controls may be insufficient if the top leadership fails to provide a thoroughgoing moral compass tilted in a positive direction. In addition to a full-scale deterrence culture, he argues that corporations that are serious about preventing corrupt dealings need to introduce an affirmative culture where "employees and managers all behave correctly and anticorruptly because they know that such behavior is right, expected, and a best practice."[10] Obviously, that kind of affirmative culture was missing within Odebrecht, Siemens, SNC-Lavalin, Volkswagen, and any number of other multinational enterprises.

A firm's CEO needs, in other words, to articulate an ethos of ethical universalism (or something akin to it) that differentiates proper corporate competitiveness from improper methods of exerting influence and getting ahead. That means—ultimately—a refusal by the head office and key subordinates to countenance the kinds of influence peddling and influence dealing that characterized so much multinational behavior before the FCPA came into existence, and that still drives innumerable de facto on-the-ground business decisions. These kinds of rigid antagonisms to unethical procedures often extends in the best of situations to travel prohibitions without permission, bans on gift giving and receiving, and solid record keeping. Unimpeachable audit trails are a must. Zero intolerance is a policy that can only be introduced and enforced from the top, with no exceptions for "best performers" and "clever" concession makers. Integrity is a goal that can only be reached inside corporations. (One large multinational made it clear that pay raises depended at home and in emerging markets not only on performance but also on performance with integrity.) It is the ultimate answer to so much of the extortion that punctuates high-level interactions between rent seekers and rent facilitators, between the political and managerial classes that have licenses and opportunities to sell and the corporate endeavors that pursue profit. As the chief of the SEC enforcement division's FCPA unit said, "Corporate culture starts at the top, and when misconduct is directed by the highest level of management it is critical that they are held accountable for their conduct."[11]

When internal corporate controls are inadequate, and business leaders have not communicated a performance with integrity culture to their executives and to all employees, then legal penalties and other forms of exposure (as under the EITI or other international anticorruption statutes) are appropriate. Ukraine, a notoriously corrupt state, made it illegal for companies hoping to compete for public contracts to do so without having already introduced codes of conduct for their employees. These

A firm's CEO needs, in other words, to articulate an ethos of ethical universalism (or something akin to it) that differentiates proper corporate competitiveness from improper methods of exerting influence and getting ahead.

companies also are required to protect whistle-blowers and to hire anticorruption compliance specialists. The FCPA, and the British and Canadian overseas anticorruption legal codes, give some extra leeway to corporations that do what Ukraine has required.

For correcting and improving corporate and quasi-public NGO behavior, the FIFA case is instructive. The US Department of Justice in 2015 charged FIFA's high-level leaders with "corrupting the enterprise." For the Department of Justice, despite the fact that FIFA's directors were not public servants, they were "victimizing" the organization and its followers.

With little oversight from any parts of the organization, FIFA's directors had put up for covert sale the rights of nations to hold football World Cup and regional tournaments like the European Cup. FIFA parceled out golden chances for countries like Brazil, Qatar, and Russia to hold those events, and the prestige and profits from television transmissions and more that went along with them. The price of a single key vote by a FIFA board member when South Africa was given hosting rights for the 2010 World Cup competition was a cool $10 million.

A revolution in corporate or nonprofit behavior is not immediately at hand despite World Bank sanctions, FCPA punishments, and various domestic adverse legal judgments. Nor have there been consumer boycotts (excluding the massive protests in such places as Guatemala and

Honduras) of illicit bribe-paying corporations or corrupt football federations. Citizen reactions against corruption have largely been directed at local rulers and local corporate bigwigs who skim and steal, not at the foreign enablers of local corruption. Possibly, in the future, many of the more energized civil society actions against local manifestations of corruption will swell in number and increase in effectiveness and, as such, direct their consumer efforts against the supply as well as the demand side of corrupt practices.

TECHNOLOGY BEATS BACK CORRUPTION

Technology is making it much easier and more economical for civil society and governments to combat corruption. Technology provides ingenious new tools to peer at and into corrupt activities, prevent petty forms of corruption, and discover cases of grand corruption. Smartphones as telephones, cameras, recording devices, and connected to messaging apps and social media enhance observing as well as reporting instances of corruption. They are sources of evidence, exposure, and explanation. So are webcams. Opinion polling and other information sharing or ascertaining helps to raise an anticorruption consciousness. But the biggest return to anticorruption efforts will come from the kinds of data mining that sort through mounds of seemingly extraneous material to offer up conclusions or leads to investigate. This form of data mining can be used to examine every contract signed between officials and construction firms, and to detect, deter, and prevent fraud related to invoicing, cluster bidding, and so on. Artificial intelligence—the training of machines to find patterns and draw inferences—will also be useful in sorting through accumulated documents and spreadsheets.

Blockchain

Blockchain mechanisms, when further developed technically, will also have a role in combating corruption, especially by tracking tangible or intangible assets in a manner that is difficult to falsify. The blockchain is an innovative method of storing data in a distributed ledger. That kind of ledger permits multiple stakeholders confidently and securely to see and access the same tamper-proof information. When parties to a transaction agree on a deal and the transaction occurs, it is encoded into a block of digital data and identified in a unique manner. Each block is then connected to the one before it to establish an irreversible and immutable chain. Finally, the transaction blocks are chained together, preventing any block from being altered, any new block from being inserted between two existing blocks, or any other breaks being made in the full chain. The wild spending from Malaysia's sovereign wealth fund would have been easily tracked and disclosed if the blockchain method had been in place.

By digitally managing bid and tender infrastructural procurement issues using blockchains, contractual procedures can be made much more secure as well as smarter. Likewise, the tamper-resistant cryptographic hashtags employed by the blockchain technology will enhance border and customs inspections, preventing faulty identifications and corrupted transactions between importers and officials. A blockchain enhances transparency, and makes chicanery more complicated and traceable. Transactions cannot be deleted once they are in the chain.

Cell Phones

Nearly 70 percent of people in the developing world own a mobile telephonic device. Even in the poor parts of Africa, the globe's most impoverished continent, the cell phone is in constant use by 65 percent or more of both urban and rural inhabitants. That means that with older smartphones, even 2G or 3G devices, interactions with corrupt officials and daily corrupt incidents can be reported—many in real time. Reports via text messaging and photographic methods can document many forms of corruption and bribe taking, and aggregate them helpfully. Such crowdsourced material is both telling and valuable; it need not be acted on immediately to be empowering and effective, and to act as a deterrent. The record will exist,

With older smartphones, even 2G or 3G devices, interactions with corrupt officials and daily corrupt incidents can be reported—many in real time.

and it can be analyzed and used as evidence, providing fodder for investigative journalism and reform purposes. The fact that almost everyone who comes into contact with at least petty corruption holds a mobile instrument means that corrupt police officers at roadblocks may be filmed, as can corrupt bureaucrats, even if not every such event will or can be recorded.

Even more powerful than photographing illicit transactions are surreptitious voice recordings of the invidious transactions that involve extortion by public servants and functionaries. Such oral material is valuable, too, when the sums involved are large and when schemes of grand corruption are involved. There may be discussions of who gets what, and for what particular benefits.

Bribespot.com, created in Estonia, receives anonymous texts in a dozen languages. It reports violent acts, coercive instances of bribery, other kinds of chicanery, and a variety of security issues. Ushahidi (Testimony) and Frontline SMS have these possibilities in Africa, and are widely used. In Nigeria, Tracka allows citizens to identify projects where state funds are being embezzled and misspent. BudgIT, yet another platform, permits citizens to unearth secrets embedded in national and state budgets, and to discern whether official projects are real and completed.

Ipaidabribe.com, invented in India, is a web-enabled method of detailing bribing by the nation's billion or so individuals. At first in English and now in all of the major languages of the subcontinent, Ipaidabribe.com receives inputs from cell phones as well as internet-connected computers. Those inputs may be of incidents or, more commonly now, are in the form of lengthy content, stories, investigations, and the like. Aggregated and analyzed, this material allows us to know that Indians pay out more money in bribes to the police than to registry officials, and how much. The site also tells us what kinds of interactions attract the largest number of extortionate demands, and who pays.

By design, Ipaidabribe.com is diagnostic and reformist. It also sheds important and welcome light on pursuits that everyone acknowledges as evil, but still accept and practice. As a diagnostic enterprise, it has been utilized to suggest simplifications to public service behavior within the permitting raj that encourages corrupt behavior. It also acknowledges how extensive corruption is, and shows how individuals themselves can refuse to be extorted for bribes. Ipaidabribe.com at one point also distributed a list of the ten best ways to fend off corrupt impositions. It branched out to Kenya and other countries where corrupt practices are prevalent and have seriously undermined the lives of citizens. In Kenya, citizens and consumers now send texts detailing who they bribe and how much they fork over. Another official government-sponsored site focuses on aggregating crowdsourced reports of corrupt dealings within Kenyan schools. Drawing on the utility of both sites and ordinary cell phone reporting, the Kenyan government even launched an official website that receives information about various kinds of bribery and graft via online forms or texts. Photos or videos can be uploaded. Brazil has a new hotline that citizens use to report persons suspected of being corrupt; the line goes directly to the prosecutorial offices in Brazilian states.

The cell phone can be employed to track and monitor financial transactions of any kind, much as FedEx or UPS can track packages step by step, from the warehouse to your door. If transfers of monies, purchases of goods, replacements of inventories, and so on, are captured on a mobile device, then few peculations large or small will escape notice; indeed, anything that goes missing, such as Liberia's container loads of fresh currency notes, can be traced and the likely culprits ensnared.

All manner of relevant and helpful data are already being and can in the future be uploaded from cell phones to centralized servers and repositories, and downloaded from official servers to individual owners. Rules and regulations can be transmitted to national users so that subscribers are no longer at a disadvantage when confronting sour-faced public servants who refuse to supply governmental services for free. Hot spots of daily corruption can be identified and avoided, and text message warnings transmitted to a subset of interested citizens. Special constituencies, or whole populations, can be polled about their dealings with corrupt public servants so that governments, investigators, and civil societies appreciate the extent of domestic corruption.

Documentation of varieties of corruption, no matter how episodic or comparatively minor, helps. Verification may sometimes prove problematic, but the photos and voice recordings make that issue less of a concern. When incidents overlap and numbers increase, there is at least the possibility that culprits can be identified and caught. Once that happens with any regularity, and corruption wanes, the piling up of infractions and the pressure that such aggregation may place on ruling regimes cannot but prove helpful. The sheer bulk of incidents and the ability to pinpoint exactly where the hot spots of corruption are will strengthen those who truly want to reduce corruption. Together they provide a critical platform for remedial action.

Biometric Innovations

Biometric identification techniques could also assist in derailing extortion attempts by functionaries, especially in a vast and populous country such as India, which recently pioneered such innovative methods. India may be able to use its advances in biometrics and artificial intelligence scanning of deep data to remove discretion from the registry wallah (clerk) class that traditionally demands "tea money" to do its job. Biometric identification methods will also help to battle fraud, ghost worker embezzlement, and identity errors. (But governments can also employ biometric surveillance and facial recognition algorithms to limit free expression and enhance control of citizens and opposition actions.) In a different advance, India can continue shifting as many client-bureaucrat transactions online as possible, with a similar assist to anticorrupt results.

In order to introduce biometric methods nationally, a government must employ novel identification tagging techniques made possible by a host of new machines. Where once fingerprints were thought to be sufficiently individuated methods of separating individuals from one another, biometric methods rely on iris scans, which are much more unique, and not capable (thus far) of being forged or duplicated. Once, as in populous India, everyone's iris has been scanned, all identities are known. Hence, simple scans at official bureaucratic barriers or at public events can allocate family payments, tax refunds, or subsidy vouchers to the correct recipients, without officials or "fixers" taking unauthorized cuts. Think of iris scans (metaphorically) as individual bar codes implanted or somehow affixed to individuals for life. No one thereafter can illicitly appropriate what belongs to a citizen.

Equally, however, the state can use iris scans as a means to control and corral protesters, and to keep populations under surveillance.

Webcams

Just as cell phones can provide voice and photographic evidence of many varieties of illicit behavior, so webcams can stream video feeds in real or direct times of corrupt encounters. A webcam—an operating video camera connected to and sending images to a computer or an array of computers in real time—adds to a panoply of devices owned or controlled by citizens. If and when police extortionists, say, stop motorists and ask for bribes, or if and when the manipulation of the bidding and contract-tendering process is suspected, webcam evidence will help to verify suspicions and also—by its presence—prevent common kinds of corrupt practice.

In authoritarian-ruled Kazakhstan, Kyrgyzstan, Tajikistan, and Uzbekistan, enterprising motorists mount dashcams inside their vehicles in order to film police shakedowns. By uploading such actions to YouTube and Facebook, they embarrass offenders, shaming them into better practices. In all of these former Soviet nation-states, NGOs receive videos of improper, sometimes-brutal encounters with corrupt police and upload them to a central server for all to see, and then scold the state. (In Kyrgyzstan this behavior can prove dangerous, as it did when a police officer realized that he was being filmed and assaulted the driver.) In Tajikistan, drivers make movies showing the police in action at roadblocks and then show the result on local television. Religious activists in Kyrgyzstan posted selfies of their battered faces to demonstrate how brutal the local police interrogations were, unprovoked. In Uzbekistan, a neighborhood group posts complaints to Facebook when local officials fail to deliver basic services—"good governance"—as expected and required. Those services might include access to energy from natural gas or electricity, supplies of potable water, or schooling.

Just as novel anticorruption uses of mobile handheld devices are being invented daily, so there need be few limits to the ingenuity of citizens and their video devices to reduce the onslaught of societal corruption as well as to make bribery, embezzlement, and other kinds of corrupt abuse less common than they now are. Official surveillance cameras that peer at citizens in most big cities are intended to enhance security, as in Salisbury, England, when CCTV cameras detected Russian operatives leaving a deadly nerve agent on the doorknob of a former Russian spy's house in winter 2018. Yet, these video streams could also be used to battle corruption by capturing evidence of clandestine meetings, such as a mogul leaving the home of a public servant involved in deciding which firms receive lucrative construction contracts.

Opinion Polling

Information gathering by survey instrument has become much more sophisticated and technologically driven globally, and especially with regard to questions about the extent and reach of, and the harm inflicted by, corruption on citizens in general and on subsets of populations more specifically. Such surveys can only be undertaken in most parts of the world thanks to the ubiquity of cell phones and the interactive capabilities that they offer. The best of these surveys, such as the broadly reachable and technologically empowered Latinobarómetro and Afrobarometer instruments, enable practitioners and scholars to increase their essential knowledge in many areas, especially with regard to how corruption affects whole populations and differentiated subsets of citizens. Without such detailed awareness, anticorruption activists and governments would be unable to devise effective strategies to combat corrupt behavior, and to target especial varieties of both petty and grand corruption. Moreover, the results of these and many other survey instruments can only be administered and analyzed with the help of sophisticated computer-driven big data methods of disaggregation.

In addition to the major barometric surveys and their analogues in Europe (and Gallup and Pew in the United States), there are several kinds of helpful general polling operations within target countries, such as Gilani in Pakistan, XP/Ipespe in Brazil, and Ipsos in South Africa. If their frequent surveys ask appropriate and sophisticated questions, we learn from them in fine detail whether and how corruption continues, and at what relative weights. We can also discern whether whatever anticorruption operations are in process, such as the Lava Jato proceedings in Brazil, are making a marked difference in perceived outcomes.

Other instruments like Transparency International's Corruption Barometer endeavor, which has been deployed in and for a number of countries, and targeted efforts by the many governance and financial polls of experts mentioned in chapter 2, provide standardized and more comparative cross-national data. The Index of African Governance aggregates a number of indicators, including the extent of corruption, to offer scores on governmental performance for all of the countries of that continent. Freedom House does so for democracy and various aspects of "freedom" across the globe. There are indexes of "hunger" and "happiness" which to some extent reflect on as well as consider how corrupt a political jurisdiction is believed to be. Even the international charity Oxfam regularly surveys to ascertain the reliability of public services.

All of these methods of eliciting the opinions of a sample of respondents or of supposed authorities elicit feelings about how corruption intrudes on the lives of citizens, or how amounts of corruption are perceived by selected businesspersons, journalists, academic researchers, and others. The bag is mixed, but it has generally been demonstrated to supply helpful, if not conclusive, information that proves influential in policy making. These methods, along with their results, are more reliable and respected, of course, when the questions are carefully constructed, indirect, and contextually relevant. That is, asking someone what happens at a roadblock is better than asking outright if that person has paid bribes at a roadblock.

There are many onetime surveys, only now possible because of the widespread use of cell phones in regions long without working landlines, conducted by reputable organizations that can also shed light on corrupt activities in ways that could be helpful to legislators, and are certainly of value to domestic civil society change agents, investors, and potential donors. In South Cyprus, to take but one example, Nicosia University and a local business asked about corruption in the wake of bank failures and alleged Russian criminal infiltration of South Cyprus's financial infrastructure. Fully 46 percent of those who responded to the survey agreed that Cyprus, a member of the European Union, "had been turned into a 'Banana Republic'" because of briberies and other financial chicanery.

More disturbing, somehow, 35 percent of those answering said that they had little confidence in obtaining "justice" through the existing court system. Another poll disclosed that 83 percent of Greek-speaking Cypriots (in South Cyprus) agreed that corruption was a major problem there, and 50 percent of the same set of respondents reported that they had personally witnessed a bribery event or some other kind of fraud.[1]

Limiting Discretion, Removing Temptation

Modern technology enables willing governments to detect and deter corruption by locating, investigating, and punishing those who are found through the efforts of crowdsourced reports as well as police interrogations to be putting private interests before the public good. Additionally, the power of the internet and the ubiquity of cell phone technology (and the growing reliability of transmission towers and network continuity) permit governments that wish to be proactive in combating corruption to reform how they do business with the public, and thus greatly to reduce the kinds of interactions between public servants and citizens that have characteristically and routinely facilitated as well as permitted corrupt behavior of all kinds.

The person behind the counter traditionally has the power to provide, obfuscate, delay, and frustrate—all in the service of private gains for services that can only be obtained from authority. In India, for example, marriage certificates are free, but they end up costing, say, 6,000 rupees (US$130), paid to touts who intervene on a requestee's behalf with the obstinate petty bureaucrat who makes his living not from his governmental wages but instead from extorting the public. "When I was departing ... from Mumbai airport," an Indian man reported, a "customs officer requested [5,000 rupees] because my wife's last name was not changed to mine on her passport. I opted to bribe because it was 1 a.m." Another Indian said that "you do it because everyone does it. ... Say you need some building permits, if you pay 10,000 rupees you'll get it in two days, if you don't ... you spend months trying to fight them."[2]

The easy technological answer to these kinds of real, daily complaints is obvious and technologically relatively straightforward: progressive governments can put all of these kinds of public requests for permits, licenses, and the like online, accessible easily from mobile platforms and other devices. Indeed, there are almost no public servant and private citizen interactions that cannot be avoided or curtailed by placing them online. Discretion is thus obviated when face-to-face contact between the authority figure and the supplicant is removed. The more easily maneuverable the platform, the more customer satisfaction ensues.

In theory, at least, all manner of supplicants seeking almost every variety of governmental response can be put online and, by virtue of that relatively simple improvement, obtain equal treatment rather than the cheating or devious denials that are common to so many transactions between those who grant the permits and those who want them throughout (mostly) the developing world. India began doing just that in 2019, to great anticorruption success. Online, decisions between a grant and a denial are made by algorithm, and presumably fairly. Because none is favored, applications cannot be accelerated or decelerated without tampering with a computer program. Obviously, such tampering can be and has been done by sophisticated programmers, but safeguards are able to be instituted to protect against this higher level of fraud. Numbers or, better yet, bar codes may always be used in place of names (which might signify tribe or caste, and could discriminate), making it that much more difficult for the algorithm to be gamed and biased.

When everything routine is converted into a machine-modulated transaction capable of being supervised remotely and technologically, the ability of a bureaucrat to act in an old-fashioned partial manner is removed. Furthermore, this modern method of providing essential services to citizens should be extended to immigration and

When everything routine is converted into a machine-modulated transaction capable of being supervised remotely and technologically, the ability of a bureaucrat to act in an old-fashioned partial manner is removed.

customhouses, making such common procedures as the slipping of envelopes filled with cash to customs officials impossible. If determining the precise category of an imported good or package is no longer decided by a human in the hall, on the spot, then the envelope becomes unnecessary. The goal is to reduce to zero the role of the easily bribed official intervention.

Even the ability of a hospital clerk to admit an injured person only for a fee, of principals of urban or rural schools to enroll this pupil and not another, or of a police officer to wave along a car with defective lights could be eliminated by the clever use of technological fixes adapted to cell telephone usage. Sufficient political will is all that is required. The major bottom line is that today's (and tomorrow's) technology enables many battles against petty (and as we will see below, grand) corruption to be won well, and inexpensively.

In Georgia, during the post-Soviet anticorruption crusade led by President Mikheil Saakashvili, corruption in universities was lessened by creating a new National Assessment and Examinations Center that administered a Unified National Examination, identifying all participants by bar codes, not names, and by such a simple technological fix, destroying the traditional pay-for-grades system that had prevailed under the Soviets and the presidency of Eduard Shevardnadze. At the same time, Georgia removed 750 of 900 unnecessary licenses and permits, thus taking discretion away from bureaucrats and easing the burden of citizens to pay extra for fundamental needs. Saakashvili's regime also vastly truncated taxes, cutting their number and variety from 21 to 6, and was even more radical in minimizing customs categories and procedures, with the same beneficial result.

Social Auditing

Battles against corruption need not even use the most modern forms of technology. Sometimes, as in Pakistan, Papua New Guinea, and the Philippines, the employment of comparatively basic and well-understood technologies can produce telling results. In the Punjab Province, in Pakistan, an enterprising district officer concerned about bribery demanded that the bureaucrats under him who dealt with the public supply the cell telephone numbers of everyone with whom they had dealings on particular business days. Then the officer dialed the numbers randomly to understand whether or not the petitioners had been forced to pay bribes. Once the officer understood the many ways in which his subordinates had mistreated their clients, he introduced reforms so fundamental that they transformed dealings in his district. He compelled his bureaucrats to issue receipts, sign their own names, and report the amounts received as bribes. The officer then telephoned clients to be sure that he had received honest information. Corruption levels fell.

What became known as the Citizen Feedback Monitoring Program was subsequently introduced throughout the Punjab Province. Office clerks, livestock extension workers, and others were all required to record every client's telephone number. Follow-up calls were made, and the various kinds of petty corruption episodes were identified. But across the thirty-six districts of the Punjab Province, compliance was spotty. Corrupt officialdom included almost every public servant. Discharging them all, for cause, as in Georgia under Saakashvili, proved too difficult. The social audit mechanism, as useful as it quickly proved itself, never managed to overtake petty corruption in Pakistan, where it persists today. When the local leader moved on, everything regressed to the mean. The power of data to hinder corrupt activity, though, was confirmed.

In the Philippines, during the Marcos and Corazon Aquino administrations, the national Civil Service Commission designed a feedback instrument to elicit reports from citizens about the activities of touts, fixers, and corrupt bureaucrats. It distributed the results of these surveys to the press, thus naming and shaming poor performing offices and officials. Further, using the carrot more than the stick, it awarded annually a Citizen Satisfaction Seal of Excellence and a cash prize to the most honest office—the one with the fewest complaints from clients. Later, the Department of the Interior and Local Government did the same, awarding Seals of Good Housekeeping and cash payments to provincial and municipal administrations that disclosed their finances transparently, obtained clean audits, and satisfied the publics with whom they dealt. Additionally, the commission and department set about "retraining" those offices and officials who performed badly on these tests of consumer satisfaction. Obviously, in those areas and arenas where oversight was particularly strong, opportunities for petty corruption were fewer (higher-ups were watching, and so was the press). Yet, given the subsequent change in the Philippines government, and President Rodrigo Duterte's other focused attention on narcotics crimes, it is not clear if the social auditing of Filipino officials has made a sustainable difference.

Data Mining

These technological advances in the service of anticorruption efforts are helpful in collecting the low-hanging fruits of anticorruption actions. But as revealing as they are, and as potentially replete with evidence of wrongdoing as they can be, these ingenious and practical methods cannot readily capture the big money transactions that typify grand or venal corruption. The major scams—the large-scale frauds that are perpetrated by big businesses, multinational enterprises, heads of state and cabinet ministers, smugglers (of guns, drugs, and people), and so on—require more sophisticated techniques that go beyond direct reporting by cell telephone or webcam, and utilize caches of big data on which the techniques of predictive analytics can be brought to bear. By constructing powerful models that incorporate automated evaluation criteria, suspicious deviations from the norm, and thus possible corruption, can be singled out for further scrutiny.

Sleuthing of an older kind—forensic auditing—is immensely important in the discovery and labeling of grand fraud. But the kinds of graft that suck the lifeblood out of a nation and wildly distort its policy priorities can best be uncovered by imaginative efforts to develop algorithms that can learn constantly from their own investigations, thereby seeking out anomalies that signify corruption. This is another potential area in which artificial intelligence can usefully be employed by, for example, scrutinizing 5,000 municipal contracts at one go to pull out those where the applicants have, say, never successfully won a contract; their "owners" seem persons of insufficient means, experience, and education (implying that they are straw persons for corrupt oligarchs); or applicants cannot demonstrate that their supposed companies actually have "real" employees (and are instead just entering bids as foils for a fixed cartel).

Even without creating new algorithms, a "low-tech" careful examination of existing and uncomplicated data-bases can produce helpful results. In Mexico, for instance, a think tank scrutinized the rolls of the nation's schools; it quickly discerned that there were 1,400 teachers born on the same day in the same year. Once these ghost teachers—like ghost soldiers in Nigeria and South Sudan, extra teachers in South Africa and Zimbabwe, and so on— were purged from the lists, substantial sums were saved, and formidable and common kinds of embezzlement and corruption avoided.

At a much more significant level, tax authorities across the globe are now able to search compendiums of prop-erty registers online to learn the names of the real, not the paper, owners of houses and flats that should be taxed in both their adopted countries and their home jurisdic-tions, from which fortunes are intentionally hidden. The real owners of more than 85 million companies worldwide can be discovered by searching OpenCorporates, a British-originated web compendium of registers from more than 105 nations and political entities. When the identities of the true owners are known, money-laundering move-ments can be reduced, and the identities of kleptocrats confirmed. The more data appear online, the more those data may be explored to uncover information capable of hindering the proliferation of corrupt dealings. Computer programs can locate patterns amid masses of big data, thus allowing machine learning to pinpoint those behaviors that merit close surveillance by humans. Machine learning can direct investigators to arenas of probable corruption.

Kleptocrats live off kickbacks. Infrastructual improvements constitute major opportunities for graft everywhere, even in the developed world. When Odebrecht, the Brazilian construction company, bribed the managers of Petrobras in Brazil, kickbacks went to politicians and other members of the political elite. But Odebrecht also competed for construction contracts in a dozen other Latin American and several African countries, bribing as a matter of course, and encouraging political payoffs. Otherwise, how (its owners thought) could they be sure to corner the best opportunities? Likewise, in the cities and towns surrounding Montreal, SNC-Lavalin did the same, with similar results and an eventual comeuppance in the courts.

Unearthing these tainted contracts, bids, and tenders enables concerned municipal, regional, and national authorities to pounce on such fraudulent deals, and to prevent them from recurring. To do so would reduce the criminal evasion of earnings (much of the proceeds from the Petrobras fraud went into overseas bank accounts), produce level playing fields for construction contract rivals, reduce overall costs to governments and taxpayers, and cut down on corrupt criminality.

How best to use the raw data of contracts to uncover fraudulent ones is complicated, given the vast amounts of procurement data that must be sifted and analyzed. In Italy, looking for evidence of graft, researchers calculated the amount of corruption from the difference between the number of physical projects completed and the total cost of public capital stocks. The larger the disparity between the financial resources allocated to infrastructural improvements and the total price that the Italian government pays for new roads, bridges, and so on, across the country's ninety-five provinces, the larger the amount of potential corruption and mismanagement there is presumed to be.

In Indonesia, researchers estimated the amounts of rice lost in an antipoverty program and, separately, quantified the bribes paid to public officials by truck drivers seeking permits. In the first case, survey data collected from recipient households indicating the amounts of rice received were cross-tabulated against the "official" reports of rice distribution; on average, 18 percent of the rice went missing, presumably purloined by those handing out the subsidized rice or by their superiors. In the second study, researchers compared the "official" costs of a local government road-building program against the estimated costs of the same roads provided by independent local contractors. Likewise, using a similar methodology, other researchers estimated the amount of bribes paid to border and harbor clerks and officials in Mozambique and South Africa for random sample shipments of more than a thousand items. If these had been governmental investigations instead of independent academic endeavors, and if there had been sufficient political will, such findings could have been converted into surveillance, action, punishment, and prevention. But at least the studies showed, saliently, that moderately sophisticated analyses of particular project areas and corruption-prone sectors of activity could uncover indications of potential fraud.

Brazilian researchers are attempting to scale up such data-driven searches for telltale signs of corrupt behavior—so-called red flags—by examining existing large databases for anomalies, computer-discernible signs of likely graft such as contractors who win more bids than others, tender competitions with few contenders, and projects with frequent or high cost overruns. They looked for these suspicious red flags in data amassed from 150,479 construction contracts worth $5.5 billion let by the 223 municipalities in the Brazilian state of Paraíba between 2010 and 2016.

The algorithms developed to seek red flags in that data set could, with time and money, be utilized to peruse any similar data set for the remainder of Brazil's 5,570 municipal or state entities—wherever contracts are concluded between a political jurisdiction and a hopeful contractor. In 2019, a key researcher working closely with prosecutors in Brazil reported that "we now have 100+ red flags quantified to more than 130,000 firms and approximately $80 billion in public expenditure in our datasets."[3]

Now that we have much more computational power than ever before (with even more to come), and larger volumes of public and private sector data and databases, the innovative experiment in Brazil demonstrates that it is technically feasible using sophisticated statistical approaches and predictive analytics to scan mass compilations of data within or across countries for indicators of corrupt practices. Public procurement data caches, particularly, are readily available in most developed countries as well as some middle income and a few developing countries. They can be explored, as in Brazil, to pinpoint anomalies suggestive of corruption in many areas, even—as has been shown—at the municipal level where kickbacks are common but less noticeable than at the Petrobras/Odebrecht national level. This is a data-driven method, in other words, capable of improving the monitoring methods of oversight institutions and civil society organizations. If large databases could be scrutinized routinely for red flags, corrupters and corruptees could be spotted and deterred.

THE LEADERSHIP FACTOR

Corruption is a systemic complaint and a top-down rather than a bottom-up malaise. That is, the stain of corruption spreads downward from the attitudes and permissive policies of persons at the apex of political, public, and corporate entities. Leaders set the tone and the stage, the persons in charge implicitly authorizing their subordinates to steal or cheat. Integrity or its absence therefore seeps into the collective societal consciousness either to make corruption an ongoing social practice—an essential (if even forbidden) component of a governing political culture—or sometimes the reverse, creating legal and normative barriers to the wholesale perpetuation of corrupt practices.

Leaders make a major difference. They signal the kinds of behavior that are desirable and permissible, and provide an ethical or less-than-ethical pattern for their fellow officeholders, civil servants, security forces, and citizens at large to follow.

Integrity or its absence is easy to spot, especially in US presidents or developing world despots. Officials on the crowning branches of political, bureaucratic, or corporate trees affect as well as influence their organizations and political jurisdictions. No one on the lower or medium branches wants to miss out on available perquisites. If others are stealing from the public, they say to themselves, and if their bureaucratic or presidential betters are thus indulging, why not me?

Corruption begets more corruption. Just as political leaders can stimulate efforts to reduce the virulence of corruption, so leaders can open the floodgates of societal corruption and decay by telegraphing a tolerance of personal enrichment, or nodding and blinking as behavioral norms and fundamental laws are breached for the worse. Severe problems with truth telling and perpetual cover-ups, purposeful misstatements, and ignorance of obvious details are all harbingers of losses of integrity.

Leaders everywhere cast large shadows; the acceptability and growth of corruption within a nation depends dramatically on how leaders position themselves: how they deal with political party needs and the unbridled (or bridled) avarice of subordinates. Most telling is the degree to which they preside over their province or nation with integrity, or not. As an example, we can look to the very contrasting leadership postures and leadership operations in Canada and the United States.

American Deviance

One leader in North America makes occasional gaffes, but tries to be ethical and responsible in his dealings with his fellow citizens, even in contested maneuvers with his own cabinet ministers. The other wallows in conflicts of interest, sees no barriers between the office and his personal financial endeavors, and selects candidates for cabinet and other positions whose ethical lapses match his own. The second believes strongly in the power of nepotism; the other is an unwitting product of a powerful dynasty, but flouts it little. One is temperate; the other is tempestuous. One refuses to be accountable or transparent, withholding his tax returns; the other is more open than his immediate predecessors as prime minister and many others, including his father. The younger leader, Canadian prime minister Justin Trudeau, may have moral failings; the older one, US president Donald Trump, relishes and extolls them, prefers to seem masculine and pugilistic, and is proud of having cheated suppliers to his hotels and casinos by declaring innumerable bankruptcies.

Many commentators compare President Trump to Mafia bosses and chiefs. But a more apt comparison might be to corrupt and corrupting heads of state such as Idi Amin, Mobutu Sese Seko, and Jacob Zuma, each of whom acted directly and indirectly to empower the greed of their cronies and followers. They and their ilk stole wildly; grand corruption on a mega kleptocratic scale flourished. Even President Thabo Mbeki of South Africa allowed his provincial African National Congress leaders to feed fully from the public trough.

US and Canadian political institutions are too strong to let even outrageous and unprincipled leaders unleash a cascade of corruption—at least so far. But coarsening the public discourse, allowing foreign powers to interfere, even circumspectly, and governing erratically encourages similar rhetoric as well as outbursts from followers and other public officials, and enables influence peddling and contests for power, if not cash payoffs. When special interests can thus be indulged or feted, and not shared because of merit, national political systems crash. There is "a moral vacuum at the heart of the Trump White House," noted columnist Tom Friedman. "Anything goes, so grab what you can," he writes cynically.[1]

Mark Schmitt, a think tank director, distinguishes between systems that invite corruption and the individual acts of politicians like Trump who "choose to elevate private interests, or their own, over the public interest." Trump's corruption, he says, is "extreme and unprecedented."[2] Robert Weissman, president of Public Citizen, an ethics group in Washington, DC, declared that "we have witnessed a stunning degradation of ethical norms," as well as the "normalization of corruption" by Trump and his acolytes.[3]

Because of corrosion by omission and commission at the top, the United States is far more corrupt than it was a decade ago. The ethos of estimable public service has been eroded to the extent that cabinet members exceed their spending allowances, flout regulations, authorize expenditures on themselves and their offices that are explicitly prohibited, and—more to the point—push the boundaries of ethical performance to their absolute limits.[4] Two Republican congressmen who endorsed Trump's candidacy early in 2016 were both indicted in 2018 for insider trading and the illegal use of campaign funds. Several cabinet appointees left office after committing prosecutable offenses. Two influential *New York Times* columnists compiled what they called "the definitive list"—a lengthy documentation of Trumpian corrupt actions through most of 2018.[5]

The headlines make us cringe. The acts behind them telegraph a disdain for integrity that emboldens others at all levels to breach codes of honor in and out of the public (and the private) limelight. "Trump's corruption," writes Paul Krugman, "is only a symptom of a bigger problem: a G. O. P. that will do anything, even betray the nation, in its pursuit of partisan advantage."[6]

Stephen Walt is even more caustic, and also appropriately cautionary:

> Once rampant dishonesty and the corruption of discourse is sufficiently advanced, public trust goes down and bad behavior (to include lying) is no longer deterred by the fear of public shame and subsequent discredit. If Trump can lie nonstop and get away with it, everyone else will start doing it too. Apart from the obvious dangers of trying to run a society where the very concept of "truth" is no longer accepted, this situation will force the country to adopt ever more restrictive laws and regulations to try to keep individual mendacity in check. When honesty is prized, liars are shunned, and corruption is less common, you don't need as many formal rules, because most people will be reluctant to risk shame and ostracism by violating the informal ones. But when liars and cheaters get off scot-free, then you have to expect everyone to cheat, and lawmakers have to keep trying to corral bad behavior by codifying every type of misconduct.[7]

Corruption flourishes when leaders behave illegitimately and in ethically questionable ways, and attempt to destroy the whole notion of "truth," thereby denying the very concept of noncorruption. Depravity at the top

When honesty is prized, liars are shunned, and corruption is less common, you don't need as many formal rules, because most people will be reluctant to risk shame and ostracism by violating the informal ones.

loosens and fractures society, permitting corrupt behavior to become common and pervasive. The center never holds, and the people, citizens, and taxpayers are penalized. In Brazil, Nigeria, and Peru, where successive regimes have enabled and profited from steady corruption, and also in places large and small and as disparate and separated as Equatorial Guinea and the Solomon Islands, both offshore homes of long-corrupted family dynasties, "anything goes."

Contrast nation-states such as Botswana, New Zealand, Singapore, and Uruguay, where both democratic and quasi-democratic leaders set an estimable tone, decade after decade. Singaporeans would hardly dream of offering or accepting bribes; taxi drivers even refuse tips. The bedrock notion of honesty and intolerance for fraud and theft, so central to the presidencies of Khama, Sir Ketumile Masire, and Festus Mogae in Botswana, and to Prime Minister Lee's tough rule in Singapore, is absent at the apex of United States' political leadership since the 2016 elections.

Political cultures are greatly determined by leadership signals, approaches and postures, and sins of both commission and omission. Reforms, therefore, can only happen when new political leaders arrive who are insistent on positive change. They do so at the beginning of their incumbencies, like Lee, Khama, and MacLehose, or at some later stage in their political ascendancy when a striking break with the past seems appropriate, like the decisive acts of Kagame. Those leader-initiated disruptions of prevailing attitudes toward and pursuits of graft may be implemented legislatively, with the imposition of new kinds of legal constraints (and exemplary prosecutions and trials). Or they can follow the exposure of peculation and chicanery by an aroused media, conscientious auditors, independent investigatory bodies, and the actions of whistle-blowers. But none of these many methods of unveiling corruption and encouraging citizen protest has by itself led to significant reductions in domestic levels of corruption. To succeed in a truly transformational manner, these initiatives need to be embraced and then championed by political leaders who can proclaim a new vision, and then sell that vision of a corrupt-free society to their followers.

Two Special Cases

The experience since the 1960s of Botswana and Singapore showcase the upside of positive leadership. The first polity has consistently been the least corrupt country in Africa (recently sharing that accolade with the Seychelles) as well as a rapid economic grower thanks to honest management, a strong rule of law, tolerant democratic good governance, and an unwavering commitment to integrity at the highest levels of political and governmental life. The second began its independent existence as a rampantly corrupted, gang-infested city-state and, because of estimable (if ingeniously authoritarian) rule, transformed itself into the least corrupt jurisdiction in Asia and one of the ten least corrupt nation-states on the planet. Along the way, per capita GDP increased from about $450 (nonadjusted) to $70,000; Singaporeans pride themselves on what they have achieved in terms of standards of living, educational attainments, health outcomes, prosperity, and stability.

No polity has done so well on those measures as has Singapore. Nor would it have accomplished so much if corruption had remained an obstacle to good governance. Botswana, by contrast, did almost as well as Singapore if its gains are compared to other nations in its African region. And Botswana performed estimably without compromising democratic values, or limiting free expression and freedom of assembly. In South America, Uruguay and Chile are the noncorrupt exemplars; both are more prosperous and better governed than their neighbors and peers. In Central America, Costa Rica stands out strikingly in an overwhelmingly corrupt neighborhood. Estonia and Croatia are likewise less corrupt than the other new members of the European Union, especially as contrasted to Bulgaria and Romania. All of the better performers are and have been better led; their noncorrupt status can be ascribed to consummate leadership, possibly in the past (as with the Nordic nations and New Zealand). Costa Rica's experience in 1948, 1949, and after, for example, was transformative.

Botswana

Khama decided, on achieving independence for Botswana in 1966 (formerly the British-run Protectorate of Bechuanaland), that corruption was the ruin of the still-young other recently decolonized states of Africa. Understandably, knowing his neighbors, he feared that the contagion of graft would spread into his thinly populated, resource-poor outpost of freedom. He knew that sub-Saharan Africa's other early leaders, like Presidents Kwame Nkrumah in Ghana and Sékou Touré in Guinea, were greedy; the attainment of independence aroused avarice among the newly empowered. Khama wanted to avoid such results in his country. Like Lee in Singapore a few years earlier, he reckoned that to permit corrupt behavior in a fragile new state like Botswana would coarsen its people, weaken their potential for growth and betterment, and make progress much more difficult to ensure.

Khama consciously instructed his close associates, public servants, and citizens never to view their national emancipation as an invitation to personal enrichment. He made it a rule that cabinet ministers and other high officials should avoid being indebted, and should quickly cover any bank overdrafts. Khama, boldly as a nation builder, said that "doing good" was his "real religion."[8] Eschewing anything that smacked of corruption was thus essential to his vision. He knew, furthermore, that demonstrating personal as well as regime integrity was fundamental to such a campaign against corruption. Central to such a vision was a decision to shun the trappings of autocracy despite his other persona as a paramount chief of Botswana's largest ethnic group. For him, unlike so many contemporary African heads of states, being a "big man" was unnecessary.

Khama lived modestly. He himself traveled by road without the long motorcades that typify many other African presidencies. He insisted that his vice president and other senior leaders of the government travel by air in economy class, unlike the first-class travel common among high officials in other African countries. Khama understood that legitimacy and integrity were core competencies of effective and transformational leadership. He also appreciated that he could not simply instruct his followers in the Pearsonian manner to avoid anything that could be or appear unethical. He had to walk the walk, stridently providing an example of integrity. More sustainably, he sought to construct an edifice of noncorruption that would outlast his relatively short reign, and it has.

Singapore

Unlike Botswana, which had little experience with large-scale corruption before independence, Singapore knew it well. Hundreds of Chinese-controlled criminal gangs lived well off extortion and protection demands, kidnapping for ransom, exerting undue influence over trade unions, and menacing most business activities. The police routinely took bribes to assist the gangs or to look away.

Lee, on assuming power in 1959 and then more completely in 1965 after Singapore left the Federation of Malaysia, realized that permitting continued corruption would undercut his aspirations for the new city-state and that any hopes he might have for uplifting the sleepy, swampy, dingy port from its colonial torpor and creating a challenging, thriving, modern entity would vanish if he could not undo corrupt practices. He knew that he was battling uphill against entrenched expectations of enrichment opportunity among his close followers and other members of the domestic political and bureaucratic elite.

Lee believed that politically as a leader he would be undone if corrupt practices continued. Like Khama, he intuitively understood the critical importance of establishing and maintaining legitimacy. Thus corrupt practices were, as Khama also knew, a curse. They were antithetical to the attainment of upgraded standards of living and income for his constituents. Compared to a host of their fellow national heads of state and government, Khama and Lee cared more for their peoples and their personal legacies as guiding lights than they did for enriching themselves and their families. They were outliers among the newly emergent political class.

"It is easy," said Lee, "to start off with high moral standards, strong convictions, and a determination to beat down corruption. But it is difficult to live up to those good intentions unless the leaders are strong and determined enough to deal with all transgressors, and without exceptions."[9] The key to Lee's great success as an anticorruptionist were the laws that he enacted (see chapter 3), the instructions that he gave to his judges, and the imperious bearing that he displayed as a genuine, hard-nosed leader of probity. But as he enunciated, he also dealt harshly with transgressors, including many vice premiers and ministers who were close to him politically. He gave no quarter, discharging friends and colleagues on the merest hint of corrupt dealings, often later proven in court. At a reception, when he noticed a high official's wife with gold necklaces and other rich adornments, and knew her husband's nominal wealth, he immediately acted to end the official's employment. When Lee suspected that the director of the national airline, a close friend, was taking payments from a prospective supplier, he sacked him. When the minister of environment accepted a free air passage plus an expensive vacation bungalow from a property developer, Lee discharged his friend on the spot. And so on. Lee knew that corruption is enabled from the top. As he said, "If the probity of the top leadership were exemplary, lower ranks would be less often tempted, and certainly rarely feel entitled, to cheat."[10]

By the 1980s, Lee's didactic leadership had succeeded in imposing restraint and noncorrupt ethics on all components of his government. He had also acculturated Singaporeans to regard corrupt acts as shameful. Like MacLehose's administration in Hong Kong and Khama's in Botswana, all three leaders altered the collective behavior of their citizens as they reoriented their leadership cadres. They implanted, sustainably, a new norm of governance that was founded on ethical behavior. Abuses of public positions for private gain became uncommon and were regarded as shameful. In a word, the efforts of these men transformed their political jurisdictions for the better. That is what committed, visionary, responsible leadership does.

Structure and Culture

Progress in the anticorruption sphere has always been disruptive, and is articulated and activated by leaders who opposed corruption not on moral grounds but rather because of the dangers to a state's developmental prospects, to its prosperity and the prosperity of its citizens, and to the legitimacy and financial stability of its ruling party. It is no surprise, therefore, that the globe's wealthiest per capita and best-governed countries are its least corrupt ones. The various indexes that measure governance all show that positive governmental performance (the delivery of high qualities and quantities of political goods and services) correlates with the diminution of corruption. Civil conflict is associated with corruption, not with good governance. State failure, too, almost always follows accelerated episodes of corruption and kleptocracy. Structural, geographical, demographical, and cultural handicaps might admittedly predispose a nation-state to poverty or weakness, but corruption is a drag without exception.

Hence, countries in the (particularly) developing world exhibiting high levels of corruption and bad governance are often impoverished because of that corruption. When countries begin to attack corruption within their ranks and improve their rules of law, they become more attractive to foreign and domestic investors, and even to tourists. Impunity needs to be banished, too, as some Brazilians and Guatemalans have advocated and labored to achieve. Lee, by upending prevailing attitudes regarding corruption, sought to show that his city-state could exit the third world and become a first world oasis. So did Indians like social activist Ana Hazare and State Chief Minister Arvind Kejriwal seek to wean their political rulers away from easy, purloined riches by emphasizing democratic leadership and noncorrupt values.

Institutions

What about institutions? In the developed world, political cultures—value systems influencing and guiding political universes—gradually emerged after long periods of leadership and followership experimentation. (One could wonder how indigenous societies in Africa and Asia might have continued to evolve, had their evolution not been stifled by colonial rule.) But, in most parts of the developed world, political institutions are now sufficiently robust to dampen tendencies toward corrupt behavior and (with the exception of Belarus, China, Hungary, Russia, and their ilk) support rule of law regimes that are antithetical to pervasive grand corruption. In most sections of the developed world, the value systems of democracy are fully rooted, legislatures and judiciaries are mostly independent and focused on improving citizen welfare, the need for and observance of good governance is taken mostly for granted, and open macroeconomic practices are expected. Finally, not everywhere, but in most developed nation-states, particularly the ones where corrupt behavior is unexpected and excoriated, executive power has largely been constrained, or at least is subject to a variety of safeguards.

Not so in the developing world. There the executive wields preponderant power, sometimes over legislators and judges. In that realm, there is as yet too little functional separation of powers and too little acceptance by the political class of the civic value of evenhanded, non-monarchical rule. The developing world is largely preinstitutional. That is, political cultures are still being nurtured. The role of a political leader is much more salient and determinative. It matters far less who governs Norway than who governs Niger or Nigeria; developing world elected or unelected leaders have much more power in the preinstitutional states, and much more capacity to enable good or bad governance. "Outcomes for the citizens of the [nations of] the developing world depend greatly on the actions and determinations of [political] leaders and on critical leadership political decisions."[11] That means, in general, that executive predilections and performance greatly determines whether a developing nation-state—a Fiji or Paraguay—is or is not subject to the curse of corruption.

Human agency alone, overcoming the influence of structure, context, and institutional robustness, guides nations into or out of economic growth trajectories, educational results, and health manifestations—especially whether or not a country experiences less or more corruption. Anecdotal surmises suggest such conclusions. Survey and opinion polling agrees. So does the trend of serious quantitative investigation.

The developing world is largely preinstitutional. That is, political cultures are still being nurtured. The role of a political leader is much more salient and determinative.

Leaders cast large shadows. They are responsible for opening the sluices of corruption ever more generously, as Mbeki did in South Africa early in this century and Zuma expanded. Leaders who tolerate corrupt dealings among subordinates for personal or party gain (as in Brazil), and scheme to criminalize their states (as in Afghanistan and Guatemala), permit flows of funds as they cascade over the cataracts of avarice. The acceptability of corrupt practices depends on leaders; the media and the courts can push back, but the signals sent from the top of the party or national political apparatuses are always determinative. Integrity tells. Its absence announces wholesale raids on the state (as in Russia or Egypt). Anything goes.

Size and Wealth

Note the scale of most of the success stories. Botswana, Costa Rica, Croatia, Estonia, Hong Kong, Singapore, and Uruguay are all still relatively small and compact states. (Chile and Rwanda are larger, at nineteen and twelve million people, respectively.) Cape Verde and Mauritius join Botswana and the Seychelles in being far less corrupt than their African peers; all are small physically and in terms of population. Certainly it is easier to preside as a catalyst for change over smaller, more homogeneous political jurisdictions even if the peoples of Botswana and Singapore are actually far less homogeneous than is usually assumed. Certainly, too, determined political leaders can have a greater impact if their political compasses are not distorted by the different competing interest groups that inhabit larger entities. Moreover, rooting out the connivers and cheaters is easier if there are fewer of them. As Deng Xiaoping supposedly commented after visiting Singapore, "If I had only Shanghai, I too might be able to change as quickly [as Singapore] … but I have the whole of China!"[12]

Being a smallish, compact island may help too, conceivably because of isolation and tighter social controls as well as sheer size. But being an island is not enough to ensure a land free of corruption. Madagascar, always questionably ruled, is extremely corrupt. So is Equatorial Guinea, dominated by its oil-rich island. Cape Verde, Mauritius, and the Seychelles are little-corrupt island states, all astutely led since independence. In short, accomplished leaders are critical. According to the standard measures, two-thirds of all island states are well governed; about half of the globe's well-governed polities are island-states.

Being wealthier could predispose a nation-state to limited and limiting corruption. The Nordic nations are wealthier per capita than most other polities. So are New Zealand and Australia, Canada, Hong Kong, and Singapore.

No non–oil producer surpasses Botswana, Mauritius, and the Seychelles in income per capita in Africa. While wealth can be a predictor of anticorruption activity, a close examination across centuries (and recent experience) reveals that reducing levels of corruption precedes, rather than follows, increasing incomes. Leaders always intervened to accelerate adherence to new noncorrupt performance standards.

ACHIEVING ANTICORRUPTION
SUCCESS: A RECIPE

Anticorruption efforts can succeed. Citizens and consumers need not passively endure the afflictions imposed by corrupt regimes without seeking and achieving positive redress. As the electoral successes in India's Delhi state, Croatia, Malaysia, Mexico, and other places show, voters can anoint ostensibly noncorrupt political leaders and political administrations, and begin to transform their societies. Likewise, protest movements are capable of redirecting nations away from the worst excesses of corrupt behavior—witness the tentative advances in Guatemala, Peru, and Slovakia. We also know that the collective behavioral intolerance of corrupt practices gradually created the globe's least corrupt modern polities: the Nordic nations, New Zealand, Canada, and the rest. That list also includes the outliers in their own neighborhoods: Botswana, Mauritius, and Rwanda in Africa, Uruguay and Chile in South America, and Estonia and Croatia in eastern Europe. Hong Kong and Singapore led the way, demonstrating that determined political leadership could turn even the most thoroughly corrupt jurisdictions into paragons of probity.

What all of these outposts of comparative virtue have done by making corrupt acts shameful rather than routine is to raise domestic standards of living and developmental outcomes, increase educational opportunities and public health benefits, and uplift average levels of GDP per capita. Anticorruption pays. Thus, removing the stain of corruption and its many ancillary accompaniments has immediate and lasting paybacks, especially in the world's least well-governed, poorer, and often fragile or failed states.

Earlier chapters in this book have discussed many of the initiatives that are and have been capable of lessening the impress of corruption. Effective laws and adequate sanctions comprise the first line of attack. Investigative endeavors of several varieties, but including commissions modeled on Hong Kong's pioneering ICAC, are salutary. Instruments of that sort develop information and prepare indictments, inform well-motivated prosecutors, and build tight cases to be tried by judges who are fully independent from the ruling executive. (Without a free and honest judiciary, providing deterrents sufficient to halt future corruption becomes almost impossible.) Ultimately,

Removing the stain of corruption and its many ancillary accompaniments has immediate and lasting paybacks, especially in the world's least well-governed, poorer, and often fragile or failed states.

however, raising the costs of corruption to individuals by beating them with the punitive bat of punishment is but a partial answer to the scourge of societal corruption.

A second line of offense of equal importance involves strengthening accountability and transparency by supporting and welcoming a vigilant, observant media capable of uncovering and detailing abuses by politicians, officials, and other corrupt leaders. Auditors general with forensic experience along with ombudspersons to receive and investigate citizen concerns and complaints are also intrinsic to the anticorruption battle. South Africa's ombudsperson (the public protector) performed decisively in that country's identification of corrupt dealings. There is a role, too, in this difficult combat for large-scale outside audits of whole countries, such as the massive examination of Malawi's official books in 2015. Furthermore, sophisticated forensic accounting employing artificial intelligence or econometric modeling can now assist in discovering likely fraudulent behavior, thereby alerting prosecutors, the media, and civil society watchdogs.

Energetic and emboldened civil societies are critical. They can act as the vanguard of citizen-wide concerns and, using social media and other new technological methods, refuse to accept fraud and graft by rulers and ruling elites. Indeed, as in Paraguay in 2019, citizen protesters can shame prosecutors and other public officials to act against corrupt politicians. Women, led by Maria Esther Roa, a criminal lawyer, surrounded the house of Senator José Maria Ibañez, who had admitted to using public funds illegally to pay employees working on his country estate, but had survived an official vote of impeachment. Roa and a horde of other women banged pots and bans, covered the senator's house with toilet paper and raw eggs, and humiliated him into resigning. Prosecutors also filed charges against other offending senators and officials, thus demonstrating the power of aroused civil disobedience—in at least one salutary case.

It helps, too, along the third line of attack, to remove anything bureaucratic that allows agents of the state to be tempted to abuse their authority. The less discretion available to such intermediaries between the administration and the public, the fewer opportunities there are to extort payments for services—to lubricate transactions. Similarly the fewer the permits that must be obtained, the fewer the customs categories, the fewer the barriers that citizens have to cross to complete their daily errands, and the fewer the everyday interactions with police personnel, the fewer the chances are that someone with power will attempt to wield it against a civilian.

Much of traditional petty corruption vanishes when polities put all or most of their transactions with citizens online. Digitizing the permit application process eliminates nearly all of those interventions that would hitherto have constituted perfect opportunities for graft. Estonia rapidly transitioned from Soviet and post-Soviet corruption to its current largely noncorrupt status mostly by becoming one of the globe's most thoroughly digital enterprises. Citizens no longer are propositioned by bureaucrats tempted to exchange a service for cash.

Each of these progressive reforms or innovations is important in any attempt to battle corrupt operations to a standstill. Each is necessary. Yet none, on its own, can curb corruption completely. Strengthening political institutions (or reforming them so that they can operate responsibly) is another relevant and necessary objective. But doing so is only part of the package of change that must occur if societies are to shift from corrupt to noncorrupt sides of the ledger. Whole societies, not just sections of the whole, need to be transformed if societies long mired in chicanery and sleaze are to embrace ethical universalism, and begin the long walk back to good governance and a robust rule of law.

As this book has emphasized, little of what is suggested above by way of advances, and little of the overall attitudinal societal shift away from corruption, can happen absent political leaders committed to erasing corruption as a customary way of life and rule. Leaders send signals to their colleagues, officials, and functionaries. Without affirming moves away from business as usual, or as Khama did in Botswana and Lee did in Singapore, without imposing a new sense of integrity on leaders themselves and their close associates, transitioning away from the expectation of profiteering at the public's expense is difficult and unlikely. Khama transformed his society in that manner without resorting to coercion. Others, such as Lee and Kagame, brooked less dissent and were heavy-handed, unnecessarily sacrificing essential freedoms to limit peculation and fraud.

In order to reorient grasping grand corrupters and their petty corrupt imitators, the commitment of the new or reforming leader must be credible and her personal deportment visibly chaste. Leaders who are compromised personally, and are therefore illegitimate in the eyes of their publics, doom any anticorruption efforts to early failure.

No winning campaign against corruption succeeds without leaders who articulate a vision of noncorruption, mobilize their immediate and distant followers behind that vision, are themselves accountable and transparent, and are able over time to socialize whole societies to accept the benefits and responsibilities of eschewing influence seeking through contract fraud, speed payments, and similar queue-jumping mechanisms. Those kinds of leaders do more than just set out the goals of a just society: they educate, instruct, and create enduring administrative edifices of anticorruption.

Few anticorruption crusades have succeeded that have not been leader conceived and driven. That said, since responsible political leadership clearly makes a material difference in these and other kinds of political circumstances, especially in the poor and preinstitutionalized states that are common in the developing world, how do we nurture those kinds of willing reformers? The lessons derived from anticorruption efforts in nineteenth-century Europe, especially in Scandinavia, emphasize leadership that emerges when publics are better educated, more middle class, more bourgeois, more aware of their participation in the global village, and much more demanding of their elected or appointed rulers. Sometimes, too, as in contemporary Brazil, Croatia, India, or Mexico, unelected, nonpolitical leaders arise to articulate and motivate anticorruption efforts that press ruling classes to reform as well as vast publics to protest and demand positive improvements. Always, there must be leadership of some determined, appealing kind. Indeed, citizenries on their own cannot cleanse whole societies of the scourge of corruption; from among their ranks, and the ranks of those they elect, they must find leaders appropriate for the massive task of constructing a noncorrupt enterprise.

There is a role in this process of societal change for outsiders, too. Even though the struggle against corruption is foremost an internal concern, using local instruments forged on the anvil of committed leadership, the heads of state and government of regional or international countries of influence, and of regional and international organizations, can support the anticorruption endeavors of developing country leaders by extolling their efforts, providing financial support, and lending expertise. Equally, powerful nations as well as external leaders should heap obloquy on those who run the most corrupt, often-criminalized nations of world, refuse to welcome them at home, downgrade diplomatic relations with them, and minimize trade and other forms of commerce. Naming and shaming is too little done among nations. Sanctions on individuals are frequently appropriate, as is confiscating the assets of egregious miscreants (as Brazil, France, and the United States did in the case of Equatorial Guinea's vice president). Furthermore, if and when an IACC becomes a forceful global institution, leaders of powerful nations can support its efforts to reduce kleptocracy and thereby improve the lives of now-downtrodden publics.

Fortunately, although assaults on corrupt practices across the globe are hardly universal and not as yet widespread, there is a brighter light increasingly being shone on corruption everywhere. The influence of social media across cultures and continents along with the almost-universal use of cell phones and the information that they transmit to disparate peoples mean that the evils of corruption are well disseminated. The citizens of polities long accustomed to the pall of corruption in their nation-states now know that they need not endure it at home—that they can hope to emulate those several countries that have broken the golden corset of corruption, or at least lessened its domestic yoke on their lives. Increasingly, the ills of corruption are being illuminated within Africa, Asia, and Latin America; corruption no longer lurks in the shadows, unspoken and unacknowledged, but is ever present as well as ever destructive of national priorities. The disease that was little discussed before the 1990s is now named as one of the two or three central odious conditions of our times. We fortunately know what the remedies are; given sufficient political will those remedies can be administered within the more corrupt jurisdictions of the planet to the immense benefit of its long-suffering peoples.

Among the specific remedies that leaders and governments can sponsor, there are a few that summarize and provide a suitable set of recommendations for a plausible anticorruption effort. Any head of state, head of government, or regime that wants at least to begin to do battle with corrupt forces should adopt the following abbreviated set of tried-and-true methods to minimize corruption within her or his state:

1. Incoming political leaders intent on reform should remove holdover senior ministers and officials who are tainted by corrupt practices, and quickly discharge any of their own appointees who lick sticky fingers or trade personal enrichment for the exercise of undue influence. They should promise to continue to clean the political

and bureaucratic stables of anyone, at any national or regional level, who abuses his or her public position for private gain.

2. The new executive and legislature can strengthen the legal barriers against corruption, and revamp or establish a new anticorruption commission with extensive investigative and prosecutorial prerogatives and a broad mandate to extirpate corruption wherever it is located, preferably on the Hong Kong model. The new executive can appoint a tough-minded, responsible, experienced prosecutor or lawyer to head such a commission, provide for its financial and personnel needs, and guarantee the commission and its head independence from executive, legislative, or crony interference.

3. As added armament, the executive and legislature can create or strengthen existing offices of an auditor general, and appoint a person with skills and vision to head that office. It is important that the auditor general and an ombudsperson report to the nation, not just to parliament or the president, and that the auditors have the right and responsibility to investigate the accounts of all governmental and parastatal offices and officeholders, at all levels.

4. The executive and legislature should bind the nation to the provisions of the proposed IACC, giving citizens

added protection and further avenues of appeal against illicit behaviors. Or a brave executive and a cooperative legislature could welcome a Guatemalan-like UN Commission against Impunity, with or without the massive public pressure that was formative in Guatemala.

5. The president and all senior elected officials should declare their assets, open those declarations to public scrutiny, and insist that all political appointees, judges, ambassadors, and civil service employees above a specified certain rank also file elaborate declarations of assets annually, allowing the auditor general to scrutinize them and report back publicly to the nation about their full contents.

6. The president should appoint life-tenured senior judges with impeccable integrity, and establish an escrow account not subject to legislative manipulation to pay their salaries, with regular raises, so as to sustain their independence and impartiality.

7. To enhance transparency, the president and the legislature should promise publicly to respect press and media freedom. Together, they should back a permissive freedom of information law, and open all government books to the media and civil society.

8. The newly established national anticorruption commission should energetically inaugurate a section

within its organization to prevent corruption, and another to educate the public about the ills of corruption and the rights of all citizens, again on the Hong Kong model. This commission should sponsor integrity training sessions for corporate as well as public leaders. The object of this portion of the commission's work should be to socialize citizens to understand that corrupt practices are no longer tolerated. Preventive efforts and educational outreach are designed to create a new national norm of ethical universalism that is antithetical to the practice of corruption.

9. A compendium of rights should be posted for public viewing at every office where citizens interact with bureaucrats and seek permits, licenses, and the like. It should also be distributed over the internet and via social media. Further, permitting and licensing activities should be shifted online, thus making the exercise of bureaucratic discretion that much more unusual.

10. An anticorruption commission should create hotlines to receive anonymous or open citizen telephonic reports, text messages, videos, or other allegations and evidence of bribing, extortion, graft, and so on, by police officers, customs inspectors, airport security agents, tax officials, or any other public servants. It should also welcome and provide financially appropriate support for whistle-blowers and whistle-blowing.

11. The national anticorruption commission should adopt advanced quantitative methods, and use expenditure surveys to measure public works programs and other large-scale spenders of public capital to determine whether state funds are being disbursed and utilized without accompanying graft.

12. The government should abolish a bevy of regulations and simplify its tariff schedules to reduce those arenas in which the exercise of human discretion encourages corruption.

13. On behalf of the nation, the president or prime minister along with the legislature should agree to adhere to the provisions of the EITI, and bring national laws into conformity with the Organization for Economic Cooperation and Development's Convention against Bribery and the UN Convention against Corruption as well as regional anticorruption guidelines and agreements.

The Cure

Corruption, the crippling malaise that hinders economic growth and social welfare, can be cured. The preceding thirteen initiatives are practical means to that oft-elusive end. None is technically difficult or dependent on elaborate designs. None is sophisticated administratively. None should upset existing noncorrupt bureaucratic and other national processes. None is expensive. Even the adoption of one or only several of the thirteen initiatives would have a positive effect since each responds to a different piece of the corruption puzzle.

The key factor is political will. Prevailing national patterns of dishonest and manipulative behavior by and within political elites cannot be disrupted easily without an exercise of political will that is bold as well as legitimate. Political leaders who have succeeded sustainably in reforming their nations and curbing corruption know those truths. No lasting improvements occur exclusively through popular action. All have come, and will in the future come, by a leader championing the spirit and letter of these improvements, and using each to advance the cause of human justice. Difficult times, corrupt times, demand nothing less.

GLOSSARY

Bribery
A reward to encourage authority to pervert the conduct of public business; an inducement to influence the conduct of a person in a position of public trust.

Chicanery
Deception, especially in the conversion of public legal property to private use.

Coparticipation
Joint participation by opposing political parties in a democratic political system.

Corruption
The abuse of an official public position for private gain; the abuse of a position of public trust for private gain.

Embezzlement
Fraudulently to appropriate public property to one's own private use.

Emoluments
Illicit profits or fees from an office, employment, or sale.

Ethical Universalism
All inhabitants of a jurisdiction are treated fairly, equally, and tolerantly. Minorities are entitled to the same privileges and opportunities as majorities.

Extortion
The practice of obtaining something through force or threats.

Fraud
An intentional perversion of truth to induce another to part with cash and valuable items, and surrender a legal right; deception; imposture.

Ghost Workers
Employees who do not exist or are sometimes dead, and still draw wages that are paid to others.

Graft
Acquisition of money, position, or influence by dishonest or questionable means.

Grand Corruption
Large-scale misappropriation of public funds for private gain; the fiddling of construction contracts in order to extract rents for persons of authority who abuse their guardianship of the public interest.

Kickbacks
A payment under the table in exchange for an overinvoiced contract or some similar purchase arrangement; a sharing of corrupt wealth among coconspirators.

Kleptocracy
A nation-state ruled by thieves; a polity in which theft (usually of natural resources) by those who wield power prevails. A kleptocrat hence is political leader who abuses her position for (usually sizable) personal gain.

Nepotism
Undue favoritism to family members and relatives; the bestowal of privilege and patronage by reason of relationship rather than merit.

Ombudsperson
Someone appointed by a government to be the point person for complaints against the state and its leaders. Ombuds offices try to investigate and right injustices.

Particularism
Regimes treat individuals and groups differently, not equally.

Peculation
To embezzle; to misappropriate public monies.

Petty Corruption
Small-scale extortion by persons of authority of citizens expecting services.

Public Trust
A common law doctrine that protects a nation's resources for the use and enjoyment of all inhabitants of a political jurisdiction.

Rents
Any payment to an owner or factor of production in excess of the costs needed to bring that factor into production; the amount in excess of the true cost or value of a product or contract.

Rent Seeking
The fact or practice of manipulating public policy or economic conditions as a strategy for increasing profits; seeking to increase one's share of existing riches without creating new wealth; reduced economic efficiency through poor allocation of resources, reduced actual wealth creation, lost government revenue, and increased income inequality.

Resource Curse
Despite being endowed with natural resource wealth, many such countries produce lower levels of economic development than deserved because their leaders focus on the corrupt opportunities provided by rents derived from those resources, fail to invest revenues (from oil or copper, say) to better their infrastructures or human capital, and end up appreciating national exchange rates and thus lowering rather than raising the incomes of the poor.

Sleaze
Immoral, sordid, and corrupt behavior, especially in business or politics.

NOTES

Preface
1. CleanGovBiz, "Background Brief: The Rationale for Fighting Corruption," Organisation for Economic Co-operation and Development, 2014, www.oecd.org/cleangovbiz/49693613.pdf.

Acknowledgments
1. Theodore Roosevelt, *The Strenuous Life: Essays and Addresses* (1900; repr., New York: Century, 2012), 61.

Chapter 1
1. James C. Scott, *Comparative Political Corruption* (Englewood Cliffs, NJ: Prentice Hall, 1972), 27–40.

2. John T. Noonan Jr., *Bribes* (New York: Macmillan, 1984), xi, 13–14, 702.

3. Scott, *Comparative Political Corruption*, 3, 21.

4. Samuel Johnson, "Adventurer #137," (Feb. 26, 1754), #1663, http://www.samueljohnson.com/reform.html; Laura Underkuffler, "Defining Corruption: Implications for Action," in *Corruption, Global Security, and World Order*, ed. Robert I. Rotberg (Washington, DC: Brookings, 2009), 27–42.

5. Quoted in "Lee Kuan Yew's Chance of a Lifetime," *Straits Times*, February 16, 2013.

6. "Afghanistan's Government Retakes a Strategic Town," *Economist*, August 18, 2018.

7. John F. Sopko, quoted in Rod Nordland, "U.S Accuses Food Supplier of Violating Sanctions," *New York Times*, December 6, 2018.

8. Quoted in Richard L. Cassin, "Too Oppressed by Corruption to Talk about It," FCPA Blog, October 15, 2018, http://www.fcpablog.com/blog/2018/10/15/too-oppressed-by-corruption-to-talk-about-it.html.

9. Theodore Roosevelt, *The Strenuous Life: Essays and Addresses* (1900; repr., New York: Century, 2012), 68.

10. Juan E. Pardinas, quoted in Kirk Semple, "Grass Roots Anticorruption Drive Puts Heat on Mexican Lawmakers," *New York Times*, May 28, 2016, https://www.nytimes.com/2016/05/29/world/americas/grass-roots-anticorruption-drive-puts-heat-on-mexican-lawmakers.html.

11. Dev Kar and Joseph Spanjers, "Illicit Financial Flows from Developing Countries: 2004–2013," Global Financial Integrity, December 8, 2015, https://gfintegrity.org/report/illicit-financial-flows-from-developing-countries-2004-2013/.

12. "The Cost of Corruption in Europe—Up to €990 Billion (£781.64 Billion) Lost Annually," RAND Corporation, March 22, 2016, www.rand.org/news/press/2016/03/22; Kwabena Gyimah-Brempong, "Corruption, Economic Growth, and Income Inequality in Africa," Economics of Governance 3, no. 3 (2002): 183–209.

13. James D. Wolfensohn, quoted in Vinay Bhargava, "Curing the Cancer of Corruption," July 10, 2006, http://siteresources.worldbank.org/EXTABOUTUS/Resources/Ch18.pdf; John Kerry, quoted in Stephen Castle and Kimiko de Freytas-Kimura, "Leaders Vow to Thwart Financial Corruption," New York Times, May 13, 2016.

14. "Congestion Charging, Congo Style," Economist, September 8, 2018.

15. UN Office on Drugs and Crime, The Global Programme against Corruption: UN Anti-Corruption Toolkit, 3rd ed. (Vienna: UN Office on Drugs and Crime, 2004), n.p.

16. "Lessons from Lusaka," Economist, September 15, 2018.

17. Quoted in Felipe Monteiro, "Leadership Lessons from the Center of Operation Car Wash," FCPA Blog, August 10, 2018, http://www.fcpablog.com/blog/2018/8/10/leadership-lessons-from-the-center-of-operation-car-wash.html. Moro was a criminal court judge before his battle against political impunity and the Lava Jato corruption cases gave him national visibility. But his decision to join the administration of President Jair Bolsonaro as minister of justice was heavily criticized, especially by supporters of former president Luiz Inácio (Lula) da Silva, whom he had jailed for corruption. Those backers of Lula wonder if Moro had preexisting arrangements with Bolsonaro. Yet, in 2019, several Brazilian opinion polls found that no other political figure in Brazil was as popular as Moro.

Chapter 2

1. Transparency International, "Corruption Perceptions Index," 2014, https://www.transparency.org/cpi2014.

2. Robert I. Rotberg, The Corruption Cure: How Citizens and Leaders Can Combat Graft (Princeton, NJ: Princeton University Press, 2017), 76.

Chapter 3

1. Anna Persson, Bo Rothstein, and Jan Teorell, "Why Anticorruption Reforms Fail—Systemic Corruption as a Collective Action Problem," *Governance* 26 (2013): 454, 458.

2. Alina Mungiu-Pippidi, *The Quest for Good Governance: How Societies Develop Control of Corruption* (New York: Cambridge University Press, 2015), 163; Alina Mungiu-Pippidi, "Becoming Denmark: Historical Designs of Corruption Control," *Social Research* 80 (2013): 1262.

3. Quoted in Gardiner Harris, "Obama Easily Warms to Nordic Heads of State," *New York Times*, May 14, 2016.

4. Robert Bothwell, Ian Drummond, and John English, *Canada, 1900–1945* (Toronto: University of Toronto Press, 1987), 52.

5. Quoted in Kenneth Kernaghan, "The Ethical Conduct of Public Servants," in *Political Corruption in Canada: Cases, Causes, and Cures*, ed. Kenneth M. Gibbons and Donald C. Rowat (Toronto: McClelland and Stewart, 1976), 160.

Chapter 4

1. GAN Business Anti-Corruption Portal, "Uruguay Corruption Report," May 2016, www.business-anti-corruption.com/country-profiles/Uruguay.

2. Benny Pollack and Ann Matear, "Dictatorship, Democracy and Corruption in Chile," *Crime, Law and Social Change* 25 (1996): 371–382.

3. Patricio Navia, Alina Mungiu-Pippidi, and Maira Martini, "Chile: Human Agency against the Odds," in *Transitions to Good Governance: Creating Virtuous Circles of Anti-Corruption*, ed. Alina Mungiu-Pippidi and Michael Johnston (Cheltenham, UK: Edward Elgar Publishing Ltd., 2018), 213–233.

4. Evelyn Villarreal and Bruce M. Wilson, "Costa Rica: Tipping Points and an Incomplete Journey," in *Transitions to Good Governance: Creating Virtuous Circles of Anti-Corruption*, ed. Alina Mungiu-Pippidi and Michael Johnston (Cheltenham, UK: Edward Elgar Publishing Ltd., 2018), 184–185.

5. Villarreal and Wilson, "Costa Rica," 210–211.

Chapter 5

1. John Hatchard, *Combating Corruption: Legal Approaches to Supporting Good Governance and Integrity in Africa* (Cheltenham, UK: Edward Elgar Publishing Ltd., 2014), 89.

2. Michael Corkery, "Graft Met by a Walmart 'Wink': Company Is Fined $282 Million," *New York Times*, June 21, 2019.

3. Katya Lysova, "Private Sector Participation in the Global Magnitsky Act," *The FCPA Blog*, May 14, 2018, https://www.fcpablog.com/blog/2018/5/

14/katya-lysova-private-sector-participation-in-the-global-magn.html; state
.gov/global-magnitsky-act; https://www.govtrack.us/congress/bills/114/s284/
text.

4. Robert I. Rotberg, "Corruption and Torture in Mugabe's Zimbabwe," *Boston Globe*, February 14, 1999.

Chapter 6

1. Bertrand E. D. de Speville, *Hong Kong: Policy Initiatives against Corruption* (Paris: Organization for Economic Cooperation and Development, 1997), 11.

2. Jack Cater, quoted in T. Wing Lo, *Corruption and Politics in Hong Kong and China* (Buckingham, UK: Open University Press, 1993), 81–82.

3. Claudia Escobar, "How Organized Crime Controls Guatemala's Judiciary," in *Corruption in Latin America: How Politicians and Corporations Steal from Citizens*, ed. Robert I. Rotberg (Cham, Switzerland: Springer, 2019), 256.

4. Quoted in the *Mail and Guardian* (Johannesburg), February 5, 2014.

5. Nelson Mandela, "Address by Comrade President Nelson R. Mandela to the International Federation of Newspaper Publishers Conference," Prague, May 26, 1992, http://Db.nelsonmandela.org/speeches/pub_view.asp?pg=item &itemID=NMS.

6. Penelope Muse Abernathy, *The Expanding News Desert* (Chapel Hill: University of North Carolina, Hussman School of Journalism and Media, 2019), www.usnewsdeserts.com/reports/expanding-news-desert/.

7. OCCRP, "About Us," https://occrp.org/en/about-us.

8. Zephyr Teachout, "The Problem of Monopolies and Corporate Public Corruption," in "Anticorruption: How to Beat Back Political and Corporate Graft," ed. Robert I. Rotberg, special issue, *Daedalus* 147, no. 3 (Summer 2018): 112.

9. Judge Sérgio Moro, "Preventing Systemic Corruption in Brazil," in "Anticorruption: How to Beat Back Political and Corporate Graft," ed. Robert I. Rotberg, special issue, *Daedalus* 147, no. 3 (Summer 2018): 163.

10. Ben W. Heineman Jr., "The Role of the Multi-National Corporation in the Long War against Corruption," in *Corruption, Global Security, and World Order*, ed. Robert I. Rotberg (Washington, DC: Brookings, 2009), 362.

11. Richard L. Cassin, "Former Chile Mining Executive Settles FCPA Offenses," FCPA Blog, September 25, 2018, https://www.fcpablog.com/blog/2018/9/25/former-chile-mining-executive-settles-fcpa-offenses.html.

Chapter 7

1. "Corruption 'Largely Responsible for Economic Situation'—Poll," *Cyprus Mail Online*, April 10, 2016, https://cyprus-mail.com/old/2016/04/10/corruption-largely-responsible-for-economic-situation-poll/.

2. Quoted in Paul de Bendern, "Insight: Anti-Corruption Campaign Awakens Indian Middle Class," Reuters, August 24, 2011, https://www.reuters.com/article/us-india-corruption-middleclass/insight-anti-corruption-campaign-awakens-indias-middle-class-idUSTRE77N4JO20110824.

3. Rafael Braem Velasco, email to the author, April 9, 2019.

Chapter 8

1. Tom Friedman, "What If Trump Did Actually Shoot Someone on Fifth Avenue?," *New York Times*, August 29, 2018.

2. Mark Schmitt, "Why Has Trump's Exceptional Corruption Gone Unchecked?," *New York Times*, September 3, 2019.

3. Quoted in Eric Lipton and Annie Karni, "Checking In at Trump Hotels, for Kinship (and Maybe Some Sway)," *New York Times*, September 8, 2019.

4. For details, see David Leonhardt and Ian Prasad Philbrick, "Trump's Corruption: The Definitive List," *New York Times*, October 28, 2018, https://www.nytimes.com/2018/10/28/opinion/trump-administration-corruption-conflicts.html.

5. Leonhardt and Philbrick, "Trump's Corruption: The Definitive List."

6. Paul Krugman, "Belts, Roads, Emoluments, Espionage," *New York Times*, May 18, 2018.

7. Stephen M. Walt, "Does It Matter That Trump Is a Liar?," *Foreign Policy*, September 17, 2018, https://foreignpolicy.com/2018/09/17/does-it-matter-that-trump-is-a-liar/.

8. Thomas Tlou, Neil Parsons, and Willie Henderson, *Seretse Khama, 1921–80* (Gaborone: Botswana Society, 1995), 49, 53.

9. Lee Kuan Yew, *From Third World to First: The Singapore Story, 1965–2009* (New York: Harper, 2000), 163.

10. Quoted in Robert I. Rotberg, "Leadership Alters Corrupt Behavior," in *Corruption, Global Security, and World Order*, ed. Robert I. Rotberg (Washington, DC: Brookings, 2009), 347.

11. Robert I. Rotberg, *Transformative Political Leadership: Making a Difference in the Developing World* (Chicago: University of Chicago Press, 2012), 6, 17.

12. Quoted in Orville Schell, "Lee Kuan Yew, the Man Who Remade Asia," *Wall Street Journal*, March 27, 2015.

BIBLIOGRAPHY AND FURTHER READING

The books and book-length special volumes listed below are all worth consulting if readers wish to deepen their knowledge of either corruption or anticorruption, or if readers seek more elaborate treatments of particular topics such as corruption and technology, how the Nordic nations became noncorrupt, or the Singaporean or Botswanan successful anticorruption experiments. Asterisks have been placed before those authors and titles that might be consulted first; those noted volumes represent either some of the more recent, more thorough, or more compelling treatments of the nature of corruption, or of strategies to defeat corruption.

Beyerle, Shaazka. *Curtailing Corruption: People Power for Accountability and Justice*. Boulder, CO: Rienner, 2014.

Boersma, Martine, and Hans Nelen, eds. *Corruption and Human Rights: Interdisciplinary Perspectives*. Amsterdam: Intersentia, 2010.

Bracking, Sarah L., ed. *Corruption and Development: The Anti-Corruption Campaigns*. Basingstoke, UK: Palgrave Macmillan, 2007.

*Chayes, Sarah. *Thieves of State: Why Corruption Threatens Global Security*. New York: W. W. Norton and Co., 2015.

Eigen, Peter. *The Web of Corruption: How a Global Movement Fights Graft*, trans. Joelle Diderich. Frankfurt am Main: Campus Verlag, 2003.

*Fisman, Raymond, and Miriam A. Golden. *Corruption: What Everyone Needs to Know*. New York: Oxford University Press, 2017.

Fisman, Raymond, and Edward Miguel. *Economic Gangsters: Corruption, Violence, and the Poverty of Nations*. Princeton, NJ: Princeton University Press, 2008.

Hardi, Peter, Paul M. Heywood, and Davide Torsello, eds. *Debates of Corruption and Integrity: Perspectives from Europe and the U.S.* Basingstoke, UK: Palgrave Macmillan, 2015.

Harris, Robert, *Political Corruption: In and Beyond the Nation State*. London: Routledge, 2003.

Hatchard, John. *Combating Corruption: Legal Approaches to Supporting Good Governance and Integrity*. Cheltenham, UK: Edward Elgar Publishing Ltd., 2014.

Heidenheimer, Arnold J., and Michael Johnston, eds. *Political Corruption: Concepts and Context*. 3rd ed. New Brunswick, NJ: Transaction, 2002.

Heineman, Ben W., Jr. *High Performance with High Integrity*. Boston: Harvard Business Publishing, 2008.

*Heywood, Paul M., ed. *Routledge Handbook of Political Corruption*. New York: Routledge, 2015.

Hirschfeld, Katherine. *Gangster States: Organized Crime, Kleptocracy, and Political Collapse*. Basingstoke, UK: Palgrave Macmillan, 2015.

Johnston, Michael. *Syndromes of Corruption: Wealth, Power, and Democracy*. New York: Cambridge University Press, 2005.

Johnston, Michael, Victor T. LeVine, and Arnold J. Heidenheimer, eds. *Political Corruption: Readings in Comparative Analysis*. New Brunswick, NJ: Transaction, 1970.

Klitgaard, Robert. *Controlling Corruption*. Berkeley: University of California Press, 1988.

*Klitgaard, Robert. *Tropical Gangsters: One Man's Experience with Development and Decadence in Deepest Africa*. New York: Basic Books, 1990.

Kpundeh, Sahr J., and Irene Kors, eds. *Corruption and Integrity Improvement Initiatives in Developing Countries*. New York: United Nations Development Programme, 1998.

Manion, Melanie. *Corruption by Design: Building Clean Government in Mainland China and Hong Kong*. Cambridge, MA: Harvard University Press, 2004.

Montero, David. *Kickback: Exposing the Corporate Bribery Network*. New York: Viking, 2018.

*Mungiu-Pippidi, Alina. *The Quest for Good Governance: How Societies Develop Control of Corruption*. New York: Cambridge University Press, 2015.

*Mungiu-Pippidi, Alina, and Michael Johnston, eds. *Transitions to Good Governance: Creating Virtuous Circles of Anti-Corruption*. Cheltenham, UK: Edward Elgar Publishing Ltd., 2018.

Okonjo-Iweala, Ngozi. *Fighting Corruption Is Dangerous: The Story behind the Headlines*. Cambridge, MA: MIT Press, 2018.

Padgett, Simon. *Profiling the Fraudster: Removing the Mask to Prevent and Detect Fraud*. Hoboken, NJ: Wiley, 2014.

Quah, Jon S. T., ed. *Different Paths to Curbing Corruption: Lessons from Denmark, Finland, Hong Kong, New Zealand, and Singapore*. Bingley, UK: Emerald, 2013.

Roosevelt, Theodore. *The Strenuous Life: Essays and Addresses*. 1900. Reprint, New York: Century, 2012.

*Rose, Richard. *Bad Governance and Corruption*. Basingstoke, UK: Palgrave Macmillan, 2018.

Rose, Richard, and Caryn Peiffer. *Paying Bribes for Public Services: A Global Guide to Grass-Roots Corruption*. Basingstoke, UK: Palgrave Macmillan, 2015.

Rose-Ackerman, Susan. *Corruption: A Study in Political Economy*. New York: Academic Press, 1978.

Rose-Ackerman, Susan. *Corruption and Government: Causes, Consequences, and Reform*. New York: Cambridge University Press, 1999.

*Rose-Ackerman, Susan, and Bonnie J. Palifka. *Corruption and Government: Causes, Consequences, and Reform*. 2nd ed. New York: Cambridge University Press, 2016.

Rose-Ackerman, Susan, and Tina Soreide. *International Handbook on the Economics of Corruption*. Cheltenham, UK: Edward Elgar Publishing Ltd., 2011.

Rotberg, Robert I., ed. *When States Fail: Causes and Consequences*. Princeton, NJ: Princeton University Press, 2004.

*Rotberg, Robert I., ed. *Corruption, Global Security, and World Order*. Washington, DC: Brookings, 2009.

Rotberg, Robert I. *Transformative Political Leadership: Making a Difference in the Developing World*. Chicago: University of Chicago Press, 2012.

Rotberg, Robert I., *Africa Emerges: Consummate Challenges, Abundant Opportunities*. Cambridge, UK: Polity, 2013.

Rotberg, Robert I., ed. *On Governance: What It Is, What It Measures, and Its Policy Uses*. Waterloo, ON: CIGI, 2015.

*Rotberg, Robert I. *The Corruption Cure: How Citizens and Leaders Can Combat Graft*. Princeton, NJ: Princeton University Press, 2017.

*Rotberg, Robert I., ed. "Anticorruption: How to Beat Back Corporate and Public Graft." Special issue, *Daedalus* 147, no. 3 (Summer 2018).

Rotberg, Robert I., ed. *Corruption in Latin America: How Politicians and Corporations Steal from Citizens*. Cham, Switzerland: Springer, 2019.

Rotberg, Robert I., and David Carment, eds. *Canada's Corruption: At Home and Abroad*. London: Routledge, 2018.

*Rothstein, Bo. *The Quality of Government: Corruption, Social Trust, and Inequality in International Perspective*. Chicago: University of Chicago Press, 2011.

*Rothstein, Bo, and Aiysha Varraich. *Making Sense of Corruption*. Cambridge: Cambridge University Press, 2017.

Rudebeck, Lars, and Olle Tornquist, eds. *Democratization in the Third World: Concrete Cases in Comparative and Theoretical Perspective*. New York: St. Martin's Press, 1998.

Sampford, Charles, Arthur Shacklock, Carmel Connors, and Fredrik Galtung, eds. *Measuring Corruption*. Aldershot, UK: Ashgate, 2006.

*Scott, James C. *Comparative Political Corruption*. Englewood Cliffs, NJ: Prentice Hall, 1972.

Shelley, Louise, Erik R. Scott, and Anthony Latta, eds. *Organized Crime and Corruption in Georgia*. New York: Routledge, 2007.

Spector, Bertram I., ed. *Fighting Corruption in Developing Countries: Strategies and Analysis*. Bloomfield, CT: Kumarian Press, 2005.

Stapenhurst, Frederick, and Sahr J. Kpundeh, eds. *Curbing Corruption: Toward a Model for Building National Integrity*. Washington, DC: World Bank Institute, 1999.

*Teachout, Zephyr. *Corruption in America: From Benjamin Franklin's Snuff Box to Citizens United*. Cambridge, MA: Harvard University Press, 2014.

*Uslaner, Eric M. *Corruption, Inequality, and the Rule of Law: The Bulging Pocket Makes the Easy Life*. New York: Cambridge University Press, 2008.

Wrong, Michaela. *It's Our Turn to Eat: The Story of a Kenyan Whistleblower*. London: Fourth Estate, 2009.

INDEX

The MIT Press Essential Knowledge Series

ROBERT I. ROTBERG is President Emeritus of the World Peace Foundation, Founding Director of Harvard Kennedy School's Program on Intrastate Conflict, and Fellow of the American Academy of Arts and Sciences. He is the author of *The Corruption Cure: How Citizens and Leaders Can Combat Graft, Things Come Together: Africans Achieving Greatness in the Twenty-First Century, Transformative Political Leadership,* and numerous other books.